This book is for you if...

- You are over 50 and would like to live life to the full now

- You are under 50 and would like to live life to the full in the future

- You feel your talent and skills are not valued anymore

- You feel unable to lift yourself off the floor

- You want to laugh out loud at how we lifted ourselves off the floor… and if we can do it, so can you!

- You want your sparkle back

- You want to shine again

- You want to be the fabulous, gorgeous 'you' again

- You want to join the gang of women standing up to SEXIT together

What people are saying...

"At last. SOMEONE HAS SEEN ME! Having just turned 50, getting a copy of The Scandal of Sexit could not have been any better timed. Livvy and Chrissie are two bad ass babes blazing the way for the rest of us who may be too fearful or confused as to how to approach this seemingly saharan landscape of post-30 womanhood. A must read for anyone who wants to own their fabulousness at any age."

Professor Jennifer Otter Bickerdike
ROCK N ROLL CULTURAL HISTORIAN AND AUTHOR

"It's written in a nice, chatty way and I like your chutzpah! Good actionable suggestions at the end of chapters too. Obstacles are not seen as obstacles in your world! Congratulations to you both – what an achievement! I can see so much work went into it."

Catrin Macdonnell
Leadership & business coach & mentor

What people are saying...

"I'm really enjoying The Scandal of Sexit. Well done to you both. It's very funny and engaging. It was lovely reading your book! Great fun. I totally agree this subject needed addressing in a book. A very worthy cause indeed. Easy to read, funny, engaging and interesting. The chapters are laid out excellently and the quotes are relevant and uplifting. The pictures are lovely and help to tell the story. Gendered ageism is a very important topic to address. I like the part about collective conditioning and the chapter on money. Your take on the menopause is so positive. The chapter on gratitude is ace."

Kate Adams
Director of News, BBC

About the authors...

Everything that we talk about in this book either one of us, or both of us, have experienced at some point throughout our lives. We have a thing about people who talk the talk but don't walk the walk, so we are just letting you know that we have walked the walk.

Livvy was born into a wealthy London family, where she experienced many aspects of high society and was invited to many society parties. She was a fashion model and turned down an offer to work as a Bunny Girl... who'd wear ears and a tail after all! Through her family connections she was often invited to many fashionable and exclusive nightclubs. She could regularly be found in the Top of the Pops audience, due to her uncle working with the Beatles! She can trace her love of fashion back to this time, as another relative was in the fashion world and she used to help him in his boutique. She was however rejected by her family, when she became an unmarried mother in her early twenties, with a struggling musician. Despite remaining close friends for all of their lives until his death, Livvy and her partner went their separate ways after the birth of their son and she became a working single mother. As a psychotherapist, having paid for her training by working in jeans shops, amongst other things, she went on to run a successful London practice and open a psychotherapy training centre.

As well as her career in media, where she is a lead radio presenter, producer and interviewer, TV presenter and producer, broadcast journalist and scriptwriter, she is also a senior psychotherapist and trained in the US as a metaphysical coach. She met her husband of 27 years, had a daughter and the family moved to Somerset. A seemingly happy middle-class life ensued, until Livvy later found out that her husband was being secretly unfaithful to her. Always her belief that "if I'm betrayed, it's over", she got divorced, becoming unexpectedly a single person again, but not for long – hey, she's got a great new relationship now! Livvy also went through four bereavements of family members in a short space of time and through it all has learnt you can survive anything with a commitment to having a happy and creative life. She is close to both her amazingly talented children but having said that, they are not children anymore!

Throughout the Pandemic, Livvy has been combining her media and psychotherapy careers to be an expert on mental health issues and has often appeared on TV, radio, and in a multitude of newspapers and magazines.

Chrissie was born in London and lived the first five years of her life on the terraced streets of Tottenham, before moving out to Hertfordshire. She left home at 17, heading back into London's bedsit land. To make ends meet she did stints of gardening at Regents Park and various councils and was a chambermaid at a Mayfair hotel. She could definitely write a book on some of the things she has seen! At 20 she auditioned to become a glamour model and was in many magazines – not great for her family! This was followed by a marriage to her boyfriend who she had been with since she was 17 years old, he was a struggling musician and they had a son together. Rock 'n roll and babies don't always work well together and it ended in divorce. She became a single mum, living in a council tower block. Luckily, she soon met her lovely husband of now nearly 40 years and together they have had three more children, bringing their family up to four. From being a stay-at-home mum, she randomly decided to train as a computer programmer, to prove the point that "mums and blondes can be brainy as well!" Chrissie was able to beautifully move her techie skills over to her media career later on, driving the radio desk and editing audio tapes, as well as being a radio co-presenter, producer and interviewer and TV presenter and producer. Chrissie is trained in journalism and radio production and also in counselling and is a soul midwife and celebrant. Alongside this, she runs with her husband an eco-building company, learning the great 'running your own small company' lessons of having money, then having no money, then having money again. What a roller coaster! Through financial pressures and the loneliness of being a single mum, to raising four children, staying loving and committed in a long-term marriage and juggling family responsibilities, including eight gorgeous grandchildren, all while having a buzzing media career, it has been an amazing ride so far.

Since Chrissie qualified as a celebrant she has had the privilege to officiate on numerous ceremonies online throughout the Pandemic.

The Livvy and Chrissie partnership has been a thread of creativity, hilarity and depth for over 12 years now, with the duo winning a highly acclaimed Radio Academy award for their women's magazine radio show, doing a crazy Michelin Chef TV food show, being on national news, writing for the Huffington Post, filming with Olympians for BBC Sport Relief, putting out a music track, presiding on the big stage and now, culminating in this book. The journey continues!

Livvy & Chrissie at the Hotel du Vin in Bristol

"Here's to the crazy ones. The misfits. The rebels. The troublemakers. The round pegs in the square holes. The ones who see things differently. They're not fond of rules. And they have no respect for the status quo. You can quote them, disagree with them, glorify or vilify them. About the only thing you can't do is ignore them. Because they change things. They push the human race forward. And while some may see them as the crazy ones, we see genius. Because the people who are crazy enough to think they can change the world are the ones who do." – Steve Jobs

Dedication

We want to dedicate this book to all women everywhere.

This is for you.

Acknowledgments

A massive big thank you to all of you who have helped us, one way or another, on our journey to this moment.

David Aston (Head of Programmes at BBC)

Andrew Butler (DB Recording Studios, Stroud)

Carl Doran (Commissioning and Development Editor, TV Sport)

James Garrett (Journalist and former MD of Clearview Productions)

Arianna Huffington (Co-founder of the Huffington Post & founder and CEO of Thrive Global)

Nick Lloyd (Director of award-winning sustainable building company Urbane Eco Ltd)

Clare McGuinn (BBC Audio Creative Development Unit)

Toby Mott (British artist, designer, and Punk historian, founder of the Grey Organisation)

Malaki Patterson (Creative Director at The Music Works)

Tim Pemberton (Head of Religion and Ethics, BBC)

Simon Rawson (Filmmaker - The Son of Raw)

Jesse Rose (Award-winning music producer / DJ and co-founder of Original Creative Agency)

Bob Shennan (Managing Director at BBC)

Helen Thomas (Director of BBC England)

Kirsty Ward (Assistant Managing Editor at BBC)

Plus

HMS Flying Fox

RAF Brize Norton

To our agent Susan Mears of The Susan Mears Agency and her brilliant team, and our publisher Chris Day of Filament Publishing, thank you both so much for your support, inspiration, and belief in us.

The Scandal of SEXIT

by Livvy and Chrissie

Published by
Filament Publishing Ltd
16, Croydon Road, Beddington
Croydon, Surrey CR0 4PA
www.filamentpublishing.com
+44(0)20 8688 2598

The Scandal of Sexit
Livvy and Chrissie
ISBN 978-1-913623-83-8
© 2022 Livvy and Chrissie

The right of Livvy and Chrissie to be recognised as the authors of this work has been asserted by them in accordance with the Designs and Copyrights Act 1988 Section 77

All rights reserved
No portion of this work may be copied in any way without the prior written permission of the publishers

Printed in the UK

Table of Contents...

Introduction	17
Why the Exercises? And why Bother?	29
Chapter 1 - Invisibility Syndrome	30
Chapter 2 - The Mysterious Case of the Invisible Award Winners	45
Chapter 3 - Connections (Following Your Gut Intuition)	61
Chapter 4 - We Start with The Mind (Stories we have been told)	74
Chapter 5 - Inner confidence (Limitation? What limitation?)	83
Chapter 6 - Let's Talk About Money	92
Chapter 7 - Loving your Body Changes	102
Chapter 8 - Hot 'n Bothered (Menopause)	111
Chapter 9 - Fashion or Style (Projecting what you wish out into the world)	121

Chapter 10 - Make Up and Image
(Enhancing what you already have) 131

Chapter 11 - Partners, Friends and Family
(Or the Art of Fighting Back – Softly!) 141

Chapter 12 - You are Knowledgeable 150

Chapter 13 - Being Grateful 159

Chapter 14 - Age and Wisdom 168

Chapter 15 - Surviving Loss (And Moving on
Gracefully) 174

Chapter 16 - Sensuality (Flirting with Life) 184

Chapter 17 - Sex it up (Reclaiming your
Sexuality) 193

Chapter 18 - Asking for what you Want
(Even though you may not always get it) 203

Chapter 19 - Shock, horror, it's not only
going on in media! 211

Book Club Page 229

Introduction

There is a widespread social phenomenon in Western society dubbed 'invisible woman syndrome'. It is where women in their 40s, 50s and upwards suddenly begin to disappear from the public view. On television, in films and in the media there is a very notable absence of women over a certain age and the older they get the more immediately noticeable it becomes. For example, where you will often see male news readers in their 50s, 60s and even 70s, you will rarely find women news readers of the same age. For men, age bestows gravitas, wisdom and authority. For women more often than not... invisibility! We'd like to say here that women of a certain age also have gravitas, wisdom and continued talent, just like their male counterparts of a certain age have, and we think there's room for both of us.

So we decided that this phenomenon needed a name, and we're calling it SEXIT, which we thought was a catchy and explicit title that describes very well what it's like when you're a woman of a certain age and being shown the exit door – at that point you are not yet invisible, but all the contributions, skills and talent that you have bought to the table will be shortly leaving with you in your handbag!

SEXIT is a feeling – a feeling like you're on the floor, defeated, in pain and there is nothing left anymore;

you're not good enough, you're not beautiful enough, you're not talented enough. You have just been defeated and made invisible and it feels absolutely horrible. You just want to cry, you want to feel angry, you want to cry some more and the questions coming are: "Why, why, why can I not be fabulous, creative, inspired, intelligent, powerful, strong, sensitive, beautiful, gorgeous? Why do you have to make me less? Why do you have to make me feel small? Why do you have to make me invisible?"

SEXIT is a howl of anguish, of loss, of rage, of defeat, disappointment and rejection. A collective trauma that needs expression and healing.

SEXIT is a scandal... but like all scandals when they are shown the light of day, change can happen.

We think from observation that when women of a certain age disappear from our film and TV screens, this compounds the situation everywhere and it becomes a norm in society for older women to become phased out in general. Many high-profile women in the public eye, such as the recording artist Madonna, have spoken publicly of their own struggles with 'invisible women's syndrome', but we know from the considerable body of research on this subject that this widespread issue is something that affects all women in all professions and in all walks of life across the board. One of the clearest places to observe an absence of women over a certain age is on television and in films. A report from the University of Southern California conducted research and found that only 26 per cent of women over 40 were cast across all media platforms compared to nearly 80 per cent of men. Just take a look the next time you watch television and you will notice older male news readers, talk show hosts and so on but rarely are there any women of a certain age. The study had examined 414 scripted movies, digital series and TV shows that aired from September 2014 to August 2015 involving 10 major media companies like Sony and 21st Century Fox.

In 2018 writer and campaigner Nicky Clark launched the 'Acting Your Age Campaign' national campaign, highlighting and challenging the invisibility of middle-aged female actors on TV and in film, after trying to relaunch her acting career after a break and finding doors firmly closed. She says: "At my age it appears that I definitely chose not just to push a penny up a mountain with my nose, but a penny that had been welded to the ground and encased in concrete with a sign on it saying 'Not this penny, not this mountain and not ever.'"

Why are so many women of a certain age having this very same experience in the world? A huge part of the problem is that for as long as we as a society continue to judge appearances as a yardstick to measure the value of a woman, it will always be women over a certain age that will get the short end of the stick, because we are not allowed to age in media. We must stay youthful. How is that for women with lines and wrinkles not being represented? Hollywood and other media outlets are due much blame as all too often they portray women of a certain age in a way that does not flatter them and most often undermines them. Women have been made to believe that unless they can miraculously stop the aging process there is no place for them, especially within the media, and given the influence that the media has on how we view one another in real life there are huge issues that need to be addressed in relation to the invisibility of older women. It is very clear that the same subtext does not apply to the lives of older men.

The late Michele Hanson wrote: "The ILC Compendium is a snapshot of the older woman's life in the UK today, showing us that many women outlive men and suffer more poverty, illness, violence and abuse and it calls for young women to campaign and make sure we don't become second-class citizens. Good, because we're not. We're the "glue that holds society together", we save the economy £87bn a year, with our free child-minding and caring – for the even older and sicker – and loads of us do other useful things, such as work, have a profession, a functioning brain and body. Some even have sex and like it. And I'm sick of being called "invisible". It's easier to seem invisible when you're older, less attractive and vibrant. And many women have been trained up to be self-effacing. But my Grandma and mother were not invisible and neither am I. Nor is my daughter and I hope she never will be, because luckily we are all loudmouths. So here is my little visible shout about how to treat "women of a certain age". Treat them like normal humans. Help them to cope and watch and learn from their experience, because I'm warning you, it's your turn next".

Melanie Joosten, a researcher at the National Ageing Research Institute (NARI) and author of *A Long Time Coming: Essays on Old Age,* says her research found many women feel more and more invisible as they age. She says: "For some women it's not a problem and for others it's quite difficult, particularly if they've always been someone who's very involved and felt they were noticed." "Ageing", says feminist and ethicist Dr. Leslie Cannold, "makes women invisible, on the street and in the boardroom and being invisible sucks". She goes on: "If we weren't invisible, if we saw normal-looking women over 50 on television and in movies (not playing grandmas), then perhaps women would feel more confident…" (Some more on the media and grandmas a bit later on…!)

This form of invisibility affects all women, in most occupations. Dr Cannold conducted a survey, with questions ranging from "Do you lie about your age?" (Apparently most do, especially on their

CVs), through to "Do you see any evidence in your personal or professional life that you are becoming less visible as you approach 50?" Here's one typical response: "I recently lost my job working in the aged-care sector at a relatively senior level," wrote Liz, 48. "It may be that turning 50 is coincidental, but when I applied for another job where I met all the criteria, I didn't even get an interview."

For ourselves, as radio and TV presenters, this issue came to light when we heard a young, female radio presenter interviewing a 60-year-old woman and saying to her: "Oh, you are still swimming and doing exercise at your age! How amazing!" We thought that it sounded very patronising and it frankly made our blood boil: "Hello! What are you saying? Why is it so amazing for a 60-year-old woman to actually be doing exercise? Are they supposed to be hobbling around, or totally sedentary?" It is so subtle this ageism used in language around women; if it was clearly pointed out to someone they could be horrified. Conditioning is just repeated behavior that we have learnt and normalised and because of this we don't see that we're doing it at all, until someone reacts to it and shines a light on it.

Another time that really stands out was when a presenter said to us: "We've got a 71-year-old woman on the show who has been out protesting with a climate change activist group – isn't that incredible!!" and at first we thought how great it was as well, as we got caught up with the collective thinking in the studio, which hooked us straight into our own conditioning and ageism. How easy it is to slip into this! But then we thought; "Hang on, what's the big deal? So what if she's 71? Why shouldn't she be out doing that sort of stuff? Is protesting only for young people now? And why mention her age? The story is about why she's doing it. It's not about how young or old she is." It is as if the conditioning to respond to age or to mention age is so deeply ingrained in our psyche that we don't even notice it anymore and first off, we need to train ourselves to even see it before we can begin to change it!

We firmly think the fact that there are not enough images of women of a certain age reflected in the media means that there are not enough role models to encourage and inspire us and also to reframe how we should be viewed in society. Some time back we were invited to be part of a Women in Media conference in London, where we gave a talk on being a woman of a certain age in the media. One of the things we said is that we can do this job for as long as our minds are still working and we are able to speak and, of course, able to stay relevant. A lot of the thirty and forty-year-old women came up to us afterwards to tell us how they were frightened that they would lose their jobs eventually - as being aged forty-five plus seemed to be the cut-off point. They told us how hearing us speak had given them hope that it's about talent and not about age. Why get rid of a brilliant radio or TV presenter because she's got lines on her face, when she has so much talent, wisdom and knowledge of the job? Surely we should be holding onto this well-developed talent and skill. We had a great male editor that time who really backed us up and totally 'got' us, but on one rare occasion, during one of THOSE journo wrangles, he said: "Don't play the 'Woman Card'". But what other card can we play - we are women! (Hey ho, stuff slips out in those intense moments!)

Older women are often shown on TV as being slightly dotty or even bad-tempered. Not gorgeous, not sexy, not fabulous and intelligent. As the writer, poet, editor and founder of Advantage of Age social enterprise Rose Rouse succinctly puts it: "The media often uses the term 'Granny' as a lazy shorthand for women of a certain age – it's ageist, negative and unfair... ageism is a massive problem in society today... and by permitting this level of granny-ism the media and others are compounding the many negative and unfair stereotypes around older women." We have to be very careful that this insidious conditioning doesn't diminish our feeling of being gorgeous, fabulous, intelligent, wise, sexy and successful. So for every 'invisibility knock' we get, we become livelier, happier, more verbal and creative. This is our payback to society – we're even louder than we were before! We have also decided not to become bitter and twisted... YES, REALLY! Everything we're talking about in this book we have explored, tried and tested and we are still doing so.

Introduction

A doctor told us that, historically, women have never lived this long. The story used to be that we were meant to have babies, have the menopause, become grandparents, get osteoporosis, become stooped over and then die! That was then, though and this is now. We are clearly living longer and longer and we've got to find a new way of living life to the full where we are all included. We have so many more wonderful years left and so much to offer the world- let's live them brilliantly, powerfully and do what ignites our passion! This is not an anti-men book. This is a book to inspire, encourage and support women in being their amazing selves for decades to come and to begin the conversation about making us amazing women fully visible in the world.

We all need role models for ourselves to look up to and be inspired by. For Livvy, she loves seeing women like Chrissie Hynde, Tina Turner and Joanna Lumley; she thinks these women are funky, fun, intelligent and still rocking – they are an inspiration for her on growing older and still being full of life! For Chrissie, she loves Stevie Nicks, still rocking and dancing her way around the world and also Dr. Scilla Elworthy, using her accumulated wisdom to promote peace. These wonderful role models inspire us.

For both of us, punk icon Hazel O'Connor, along with Sarah Fisher and Clare Hirst who are both successful musicians in their own right, are fun and fab role models. They create fantastic music together as the Bluja Project, and often came and played live on the show in the studio... so talented, so raucous, such fun, and such great energy. Women of a certain age being outrageous - really!

Livvy & Chrissie and Hazel O'Connor with Bluja plus Sarah Fisher

We need to see women of a certain age in the public eye and in the media, challenging our beliefs about

Introduction

what we can and cannot do. So if we find ourselves saying: "Oh, a woman of my age can't do that!", then we need to really question it. Except maybe wearing a mini skirt the width of a belt! But having said that, if it looks or feels fab go for it!!

Madonna said recently that people in the music industry have always tried to silence her for many reasons like not being pretty enough, or talented enough and since she has passed sixty years of age, it's that she is now not young enough. This woman has been named the most successful artist in the sixty-year history of U.S billboard and we love that she is constantly reinventing herself and still performing on massive stages across the world - definitely a positive message that we can all follow in that: we are never too old to change and go for something new. We don't want to be put to sleep until we die. We don't want to accept that we should decline quietly, just be parents, grandparents, have your hair only in a bob, not paint your nails, quit the high heels, the red or shocking pink lippy and disappear behind the scenes... oh no, no, no!

We have been ignored, patronized, dismissed, diminished, shamed and put in a box that is far too small... but through it all, like phoenix's rising from the ashes, we have held on to the belief that we would never give up. We feel that if you don't put yourself out there, you will never build up your courage. Putting yourself out there means you will fail... it's the picking yourself up and keeping on going that builds the inner strength! We have cried, lain on the floor (both physically and metaphorically) and then picked each other up - normally with some quite insulting humour! Now for us this book is about egging you on and supporting you in allowing your phoenix to rise up from the ashes to where it belongs.

We've added lots of stories from our media career, not because this is a problem that only exists in the media world, but because the media world is complicit in compounding the problem and so we think it is only appropriate we add some of our own stories from media experiences. We also truly hope these stories will add a sprinkling of stardust, fun and humour to the book, as well as giving some insights and encouragement into ways you could perhaps make changes or become more vocal or visible in your own life.

Why the Exercises? And why Bother?

When we decided to write this book, we realised pretty early on that we can intellectualize things till the cows come home, but to actually connect deeply with the topics addressed - to fully understand, feel and experience each topic deeply - we all need a quiet reflective space where we can take the time to get in touch with ourselves. Therefore, each chapter of the book has an exercise attached so you can fully understand, experience, feel emotionally - and even maybe spiritually - what the essence of the words are and what they truly mean for you. This is where real change and transformation can happen. It is an inside job after all. You have a deep reservoir of wealth inside of you, from which you will find your own experience and version of each subject – images, action, ideas; feelings of joy, sadness, happiness, excitement - whatever emerges from each of the exercises in this book will be yours to keep forever.

Chapter 1
Invisibility Syndrome

We have talked to, interviewed and chatted to all sorts of women of a certain age - friends, colleagues, neighbours, even women at the hairdressers and in the street; everywhere in fact (including trains, boats and planes!). We have asked them all "are you experiencing a feeling of becoming invisible as you age?" Research shows that women can start to experience the beginning of the 'invisible woman syndrome' from about the age of 45 years old. So, if you've reached that age or over, we think it's worth asking some searching questions:

What happens for you emotionally when you reach the age of forty-five onwards and you start to feel invisible?

How does that make you feel? Does it feel demeaning and damaging to your self-esteem? Is it hard to stay positive about yourself in the world?

Maybe even sometimes you may feel like it's all too much. We are now older.... so how do we deal with what's being given to us from the world and turn it on its head? We had to ask ourselves that question when a music track we had written, performed and produced called 'Hot 'n Bothered', an anthem for women of a certain age, was denied airtime by our own station, as other presenters in other stations had been allowed... it just didn't make any logical sense to us why this would happen. The music track came about because Livvy had been chatting to the renowned composer and conductor Charles Hazelwood about coming on the radio show. It so happened that at that time he was putting on a concert which was a mix of classical and modern music and it included a rapping competition. He made a deal with Livvy that he and Adrian Utley (of the band Portishead) would come on the show and write and perform a rap song together to promote the competition, as long as we wrote and performed one as well - live on air! Livvy, in her usual 'let's go for it way' said "Yes" - much to Chrissie's horror!

Charles Hazlewood Award Winning Conductor

It was Charles's idea to mix up classical and rap music and create a national music competition, with the Super Furry Animals band making the backing track for the raps and he proceeded to send us the backing tracks for us to use with our own rap song. Firstly though, the rap had to be written!

We were on the phone as usual and Chrissie was moaning about her period pains and suddenly Livvy got really excited and started coming out with lyrics such as "We're women of a certain age... we've got hormonal rage... we get hot...hot...hot... and you get bothered. Don't worry, Bro we're not your mother". So... the song was written and then somehow it had to fit into this extraordinary music.

The day finally came however and do remember, this was live in the studios, not a pre-record – when we had to perform it. So picture this: we had Charles Hazlewood of Radio 2 fame, renowned composer and conductor extraordinaire and mega-cool musician and producer Adrian Utley of supergroup Portishead fame... and US!

Adrian Utley of the band Portishead

Terror? What terror?

But we did it, live on air. We survived but unbeknown to us, it was being filmed and the film was sent all around the BBC news and radio teams where we worked. When we walked in a few days later to work (and in order to get to the radio section we had to walk the whole length of the newsroom) we thought: "why is everyone smiling and laughing...?" We had no idea until we got to our desks... and then found out that it was thanks to our editor. And because of that support, two years later we recorded it professionally with Pee Wee Ellis, the iconic saxophonist who used to play with James Brown and some amazing young musicians and an incredible backing singer. We even had cameos from some top politicians at the time, Ed Miliband and Sir Nick Clegg. Later on, we even got to perform it at the House of Lords on International Women's Day, where we met the delightful Lord Eames OM, who later supported charity campaigns we were involved in.

Livvy & Chrissie and Lord Eames OM at the House of Lords

Invisibility Syndrome

Livvy just leaving the House of Lords

Chrissie at the House of Lords

We thought the finished track was great fun, not to mention pretty sexy, but... what do you know... we were not allowed to play it on air! The word 'nepotism' was thrown around, but we knew we were just too close to the edge... after all, women of a certain age rarely rap and they certainly do not talk about hormonal rage and about how it impacts other people. Not only that, the lyrics could be perceived as too sexy in saying "Don't worry Bro, I'm Not Your Mother". After all that hard work you can imagine how much we were discouraged, downhearted, despondent and bemused... not to mention pretty fed up. We had put a lot of time and effort into the track and had some great musicians working on it and we wanted it to be out there on the air. We had played it to a lot of women and they had loved it.

So how did we turn it on its head?

One day we had the idea of going into talks with a film crew and the BBC Sport Relief producers themselves; to get a film made of us getting fit and fabulous and using our track as the backing track. Now we have to say neither of us is athletic but hey, we decided that didn't matter... stupid us! It took a lot of chutzpah, emails, phone calls, patience, persuasion and persistence. At first the BBC Sport producers didn't want the track to be used but eventually... success!!

Invisibility Syndrome

We were filmed with Olympian swimmer and Gladiator Sharon Davies MBE putting us through our paces in the gym; Olympic gold medal winner sprinter Ewan Thomas and Olympic bronze medal winner sprinter Katherine Merry teaching us how to run; and ex-captain of the Welsh rugby team and TV pundit Jonathan Davies teaching us some rugby and how to tackle. Can you imagine it? Livvy was wearing platform trainers so she could be nearly the same height as Chrissie – try tackling in those! And try getting Chrissie to get up off the floor to get into a tackle position. It's a long way up to standing! We went to RAF Brize Norton and we were shown how to jump from 125 feet in practice for parachuting, (boy, they were gorgeous, think of the film 'An Officer and a Gentleman'... that's what got Livvy to jump) and on top of that we marched with the Royal Navy squadron HMS Flying Fox in 5-inch heels...ouch! We even took the salute which made us cry. Finally, we were invited to the national BBC studios at Salford, Manchester to the hallowed grounds of the Match of the Day studio to make the film with Gary Lineker, Alan Shearer and Jermaine Jenas, whilst our music track played in the background and the film crew were cracking up laughing. So the story went from glass half empty to glass half full: the music track became the backing music to the film and we got it out there. And if we can turn things around, so can you. In whatever job or walk of life you're in, there's something you can do to flip it on its head, to speak out, to not be invisible.

Livvy & Chrissie and Olympian Sharron Davies MBE filming for Sport Relief

Livvy & Chrissie and Olympian Sharron Davies MBE

Livvy & Chrissie and Olympians Iwan Thomas MBE and Katharine Merry

Livvy & Chrissie and Olympian Iwan Thomas MBE

Livvy marching with HMS Flying Fox - in high heels!

Chrissie marching with HMS Flying Fox – also in high heels!

The thing is, as we get to this age, we come gradually into unknown territory - we're in unchartered waters. How do we live the rest of our lives to the full? What is the superglue... the fixer... that mends the defeats in life? Is it like old saggy knicker elastic or is it something that pings back? Now it is the time to feel, to really take stock and step into your power with all your life wisdom to back you up.

We do not die from our feelings. We have been through it all and survived... and we are still surviving. In fact, more than surviving, we are living life to the fullest. When you've been seriously knocked down or made to feel bad by someone else, our motto is that the truly best revenge is to have a happy life. So how do we find the energy and focus to turn things on their head? What is the spark... the flame... that will re-ignite your passion for life? This exercise will help you find that spark of passion deep inside of yourself. It's still there, it always will be. It just may be temporarily lost or forgotten about or having a sleep. It is now your time to remember.

_____

Exercise 1

Choose a quiet moment.

Make yourself comfortable and have a pen and paper close by.

Close your eyes now and relax.

Take three deep breaths... in... and out... one in... and out... one in... and then out.

Imagine now that you are next to a beautiful crystal-clear turquoise lake and that as you are looking into its beautiful waters, you can see that something is glinting in the depths.

You are irresistibly drawn to it; you allow yourself to swim down towards it and you find you can easily breathe underwater.

This glinting jewel seems still so far away. You go deeper and deeper and as you go you can see the treasure getting brighter and brighter.

At last you can reach out and grasp it. You start to feel full of life, full of energy. Allow yourself to really feel that. Take your time here and enjoy this feeling.

Take your jewel and slowly start to swim easily back up to the surface. Lay on the side of the lake in the sunshine holding your glinting jewel.

Now it's time to let yourself come back to the room...

Before you open your eyes take your time to look at your multi-faceted jewel...

What does it look like...?

What colour is it...?

How does it make you feel...?

Take some slow deep breaths... in... out... now and slowly open your eyes.

Now write down three things you found out about your jewel.

You could now draw your jewel and write the words of how it made you feel, so that daily you can look at it and remind yourself that you have a jewel inside of you.

When you feel defeated or deflated, remember your jewel and see it in your mind's eye.

Let it remind you that you are a beautiful, passionate, creative and vibrant human being, with lots to give and much still to experience.

You can listen to this exercise on SoundCloud by scanning the QR code

Chapter 2
The Mysterious Case of the Invisible Award Winners

The whole world can be in the same dream, under the same spell... a bit like the Emperor who had no clothes on and everyone had to believe that he was dressed, except for one child who saw that he was naked; maybe it's a bit similar for certain age women to suddenly be clothed in an invisibility cloak, which is really handy if you are Merlin or Harry Potter or in some magical fairytale... but not great if you live in the media world.

Our research into why this happens all leads to the same point - that it is the 'male gaze' that defines invisibility. What is this 'male gaze' you may ask? It's when you as a woman feel defined by a male perspective on age, beauty, and talent, and it is placed upon you – do you fit the picture? This is tricky because if men have been trained to believe their conditioning that beauty equals youth, then there is a problem. Like the Emperors cloak the rest of society follows suit - hence the phrase 'Collective Conditioning'. In our own small way, we are trying to shed a bit of light on this thinking and bring in more awareness.

Talking about her fear of becoming invisible as she hit 50, the writer Ayelet Waldman said in an interview: "I have a big personality, and I have a certain level of professional competence, and I'm used to being taken seriously professionally. And suddenly, it's like I just vanished from the room. And I have to yell so much louder to be seen." Our point is that when media does not reflect women over 50 as a norm, we are all in trouble. We need to see images of women ageing out there, so that all ages of women can identify and feel validated. Why is having a woman on screen or in a magazine with lines and wrinkles so frightening… is it a fear that each line on our face shows a life well-lived, a wealth of experience and knowledge? We look back to when we were in our twenties and thirties and ask ourselves the question – were we more malleable then due to our innocence and naivety? We came to the conclusion that we were, definitely, and that as we're getting older, we're getting more bolshie, more confident, and stronger in our thinking as we have lived longer and know more. Maybe that's a bit scary for people? Having said that we have always listened to our editors and producers (unless we felt they were incorrect!).

We are not megalomanic enough to believe we can change society (shame!). We are however trying to change how media portrays women of a certain age and bring some awareness to what is going on; the first step in any change is to have awareness. Maybe just have a think… are you rejecting or feeling offended by women of a certain age on a TV show, or in magazines? If so, ask yourself the question:

The Mysterious Case of the Invisible Award Winners

"is it because I'm programmed and conditioned to do this?" Or are you so used to not seeing them, except perhaps portrayed as a caricature, that you don't even notice they are missing? If we eradicate all women over 50 from our screens and magazines and radio shows, we are losing the hope and vision for young people to age well and joyfully.

This book has been written because we feel passionate that it is now time for the whole media industry to drop its obsession with youth – what we call 'Youth-ism' – and embrace the true diversity of society, not airbrush a whole vibrant, beautiful, intelligent, and creative part of it out! It's the beginning of bringing awareness to a hidden subject: The Mysterious Case of the Invisible Women of a Certain Age on our TV screens, radio airwaves and magazines!

And so… that leads us nicely on to The Mysterious Case of the Invisible Award Winners ("dun dun dunnnn…").

It all began one day at Radio 2! We were fortunate enough to have the then editor Bob Shennon give us some mentoring and we were in his office when, being women of a certain age, we dared to ask: "So… when will we be working here?" To which he replied: "When you win a Sony" and proceeded to show us all his previous awards (which to be honest looked like bits of plastic but were obviously worth their weight in gold!).

At this point Livvy piped up and said: "Do we have to win Gold to get a show here?", to which he replied: "No, you just have to be nominated."

Now for those of you who don't know, we are talking about the highly competitive and prestigious annual Radio Academy Awards, previously known as The Sony's, which are sort of the radio equivalent of the Oscars. There are lots of categories but the most competitive is the Best Entertainment category which would of course be our category! What's more only five of the top shows in the UK will be nominated.

Challenge on!!!

As we left his office we said to Bob:" See you at the awards when we're nominated." He looked bemused but unknown to him, if you lay down a gauntlet to Livvy and Chrissie, we are going to pick it up.

"It can't be that hard to get a nomination..." we chatted on the train, "all we have got to do is to collate the year's shows and put our best interviews and bits together, and then put it all in a reel - job done!"

"Hold the vision...!"

The thing about vision though is that you forget just how much work is involved in achieving it; you just have the goalposts in mind... but having said that we have a great work ethic and just got on with it.

Back in Bristol, things didn't quite go as planned – our then editor Tim, in true editor fashion, said "NO not this year". Hold on, Tim, we have a vision. Well, we didn't actually tell him this as there had been enough raised eyebrows from him on other topics so in self-preservation mode we kept quiet - meanwhile plotting that he would have to say YES next year.

Perseverance, persistence, and sheer hard work followed but finally, the year after, he agreed and so there we were staying up nearly all night for what seemed like weeks, listening to ourselves rabbiting on, getting to the point where you eventually lose the ability to know what's good and what isn't. Eventually we got a year's worth of shows down to the best bits and weaved them together with the help of our lovely assistant editor, Kirsty. And so off it went to be judged along with hundreds and hundreds of other shows.

Well, it takes ages before you hear if you are nominated and so, after the initial excitement, we sort of forgot about it. And to be honest it was a real longshot that two women of a certain age who came into media at a time when a lot of women are being made to leave it, would get nominated for the most prestigious award there is in radio in the U.K.

So – always on the lookout for an opportunity – when the day of the announcement as to who was nominated came round, where were we but in the offices of the Countryfile producer upstairs, after having been recommended by John Craven for the meeting, trying to convince - or inspire him - in the thinking that women in the country also liked fashion and had pink nails and traipsed through mud and therefore we would be ideal for his new presenter position.

We all got on brilliantly; he loved our radio show, but we could see that bringing in our quirky humour and fashionista ideas was a Countryfile model that he could not get his head round. So, we didn't convince him unfortunately, although he did make us laugh when he said he'd heard Chrissie say on the radio show that when she was lying, she always looked people directly in the eye as a decoy, and that he was therefore on the lookout for her looking very sincere on everything he said! The thing is with us that sometimes on the show the question is: are we being actresses or are we being ourselves? Hard for people to work out but best we can say is that we can be very serious and authentic - but in the right setting!

The Mysterious Case of the Invisible Award Winners

Livvy & Chrissie and John Craven

Anyway, we came back down to the newsroom and walked in, oblivious and laughing about the meeting we had just had. We started walking down the big newsroom to our desks as we had work to do and realised that all the TV crews, journalists and presenters were standing smiling at us.

"What's going on?" we wondered. We did get on with most people, but this was bizarre and slightly terrifying.

Suddenly, our Head of Programmes, David Aston, who had been our mentor there, shouted "You've been nominated!" Livvy shouts out loud, and Chrissie freezes - she cannot move. Livvy tries to drag her by her scarf down the newsroom only to realise that she is not moving at all, she is like a statue, and what's more she is beginning to cough as she gets strangled by the scarf.

Anyway, we finally got our heads around it and checked out who the other nominees in our Category were – well, it turns out they included Dermot O'leary and Greg James... so no pressure there then.

Dermot actually sent us a lovely tweet just before the Awards wishing us 'Good Luck' – what a gentleman! Sorry you didn't get an award, Dermot, you do a great show.

So anyway, off we go to London for the awards, staying in an okay-ish hotel – after all, it is on BBC budget!! The awards ceremony was in one of those decadent hotels in Park Street, London, that had seen better days – picture long staircases sweeping into a ballroom, with white tablecloths on all the tables each with a slightly over-the-top floral centerpiece that you had to talk around. Dinner was served - but how do you eat whilst waiting for your category to be announced and the ceremony goes on... and on... and on... oh well, a good way to diet.

Chris Evans was the main presenter of the evening, bringing his son along for the ride; eventually we get to Best Entertainment Category, but we are zoning out by then. Then we hear we have won Bronze! We are shocked and delighted - all these other amazing people and we did it! Our editor sends us champagne – now's the time to drink and eat and party.

The Mysterious Case of the Invisible Award Winners

The Kaiser Chiefs play a great set until lead singer Ricky gets carried away and jumps off stage onto a table, sending the aforesaid centrepiece flying. Anyway, the rest is just slightly drunken gossip...

As we go off to the bar at this point, Radio 1's Greg James, who had won Gold, approaches Livvy and says: "I thought you were going to win." Unfortunately, drink makes her say it as it is, and she responds by saying: "So did I." Well, she managed to collect herself and congratulate him. Greg, if ever you read this, here's a message from Livvy: "Greg - I am so sorry, what can I say apart from the best person got Gold, and that champagne goes to my head!"

There were of course a few minor mishaps before getting home, with Chrissie having one too many Proseccos and dancing round her handbag with abandon, and then getting locked out of the hotel room in the morning. Well we had only had 2 hours sleep - what can you expect at any age, let alone women of a certain age! It was a bit stressful though, as we were due to speak on our station's breakfast show about the award at that very moment.

We finally got back safely and with our very own award, looking forward to a bit of acknowledgement and maybe even work... and this is where the Mystery of the Invisible Award Winners starts.

Because... apart from a celebration tea and cake

at work, and a piece in the local paper, we got no accolades or recognition at all – which was very unusual as there were lots of stories in the papers about it and all the more surprising as The Guardian newspaper had been running a radio piece on the Radio Academy Awards for weeks, bemoaning the lack of diversity, especially the lack of women's voices and there we were, two women, women of a certain age at that, and a duo no less which was unusual, beating Dermot and all the other superstar DJ's, but not getting even a mention. Our then manager Caroline did write to them but to no avail.

We got not one mention anywhere in all the press write-ups of the Awards. You'd think it would be worth a line or two somewhere!

Yes - the invisibility cloak strikes again!

So, what does it take to remove the cloak? Winning a prestigious, highly coveted, and competitive national award didn't seem to do it. We did think about doing a Lady Godiva outside all the main tabloids just to get noticed, but it was a bit cold, so we didn't bother. And just in case you were thinking of doing it, it's hard riding a horse naked.

Although saying that we did get one lovely email saying 'Hats Off to The Great 12 O'clock Show' from someone called James. We immediately assumed it was from James who was our Broadcasting Assistant sometimes, and we thought "how thoughtful and sweet of him". Then when we googled the full name, we realised it wasn't him at all, and that it was none other than James Harding, the then head of BBC News. This has always stood us in good stead, not knowing who was who. Having said that, we were really happy to get this acknowledgment and respect.

The job at Radio 2 never materialised due to fixed schedules and lots of other more established presenters wanting any gaps that arose, but Bob did give us a fantastic mentor in Helen Thomas – more about that in the next chapter. And so we set off on another adventure producing and presenting a live cooking TV show, where 'Chrissie can't cook', and 'Livvy won't cook' and we used various kitchen tools and equipment as electric guitars. But that's another story altogether.

Livvy & Chrissie and Greg James of R1 at the Radio Academy Awards

Livvy & Chrissie Radio Academy Awards Celebration with Editor Tim Pemberton

Livvy & Chrissie with RAA Bronze award

Okay, this might not sit well, oh reader, but… we do have a part in the invisibility trap. It's in the way that we deal with the situations and how we buy into them, allowing people to make us invisible or silence us; and in the way that we don't have the courage to stand our ground and say: "HOLD ON" or "THIS IS MY POINT".

What is it in our DNA that stops us from fighting back? Well actually we know what's in our DNA but we're not cavewomen anymore needing a hunter-gather as we did then. So, time to stand our ground!

The art of recovery is not an easy path; it takes a willingness to face your inner demons and weaknesses. It's much easier to point the finger outside - and often it is accurate to do so - but there is also a part we have to play in looking deep inside ourselves and making changes to the way we operate in the world.

How can you reaffirm in yourself everything that you have felt has been silenced in you? Every time you get really knocked and you are saying "oh, I don't have any talent"; "I don't have enough inspiration"; "I'm too old, I should be 30 to do this."; "I don't think I'm good enough"; "I'm invisible", "It's so hard, what's wrong with me?"; "maybe I should quit" or any other defeating statements you make about yourself, then that's the time you have to go deep, deep, deep inside of yourself and remember your own talents and strengths and start asking some pointed questions of yourself.

Here is an exercise to support you do that.

_____

Exercise 2

Take 15 minutes to sit somewhere where you will not be disturbed. Have a pen and paper with you. Firstly, start to allow your body to relax; pile a load of cushions behind you so that you can sit up comfortably and straight.

Start to notice your breathing... no pressure, no right or wrong, just noticing your breathing... breathing in... breathing out...

Allow your breath to calm down. If you lose concentration just come back to the breath...

We are going to sit for a few minutes watching the breath.

Now ask yourself: "Who or what has silenced me?"

If you feel anxious or nervous this is the time to be brave.

Ask yourself again: "Who or what has silenced me?"

Wait for the answers to come to you...

Open your eyes and write them down.

When you have written them down, close your eyes and come back to following your breath...

breathing in... breathing out... breathing in... breathing out...

Allow your body to relax...

Ask yourself: "Who has made me invisible? How did they do it?"

Take a few more deep breaths in and out and wait for the answers...

When you are ready open your eyes and write them down.

Look at your lists.

As you look at your lists, this is the time to connect with your anger and your indignation

Allow your anger to grow.

Allow it to be powerful.

Allow it to be strong.

Allow it to give you the strength and the power to make sure that this won't happen again.

Take your list and write alongside each message of where you've been silenced or where you've been made to feel invisible and silenced:
"NO, I WILL NOT ALLOW THIS!".

A WARNING: this anger and indignation is for your private use ONLY. Anger is a powerful tool - when transformed it creates assertion and confidence.

You can listen to this exercise on SoundCloud by scanning the QR code

Chapter 3
Connections (Following Your Gut Intuition)

Most successful people in the world all talk about the gut feelings or intuition they've had and their response to situations or to other people or to the natural world, and how they have often followed their gut intuition more than their logical mind. We call it the Yellow Brick Road, where you just follow where the energy takes you. You do have to be brave and take a risk and follow the connections that may present themselves, even if you don't understand it logically – you're not being illogical, you are just following a different avenue of energy and a different part of your insight.

If you go along with it, you will never know where it's going to take you – life becomes an adventure. You can achieve great things – goals you never thought you could aspire to, you reach. And suddenly other paths open up for you leading in directions that maybe you always dreamed of but never thought you could truly achieve. It takes courage and conviction to follow your gut intuition, and to trust that you are going in the right direction. Life stays safe and limited however when you ignore that inner voice. If you feel feelings of boredom, everything is a bit dull, a bit grey, a little depressing, the word 'shutdown' comes to mind –

then you have closed the avenue to hearing what your gut intuition is telling you.

Jack Canfield, the inspirational teacher says: "Trust your gut feeling about things... listen to what others are saying and look at the results of your actions. Once you know the truth, you can set about taking action to improve. Everyone will be better for it."

Raven Ishak and Jay Polish wrote: "Learning to listen to your gut feeling has a lot to do with trust." So, it's all about being brave enough to trust yourself and knowing that your instincts are correct. This will take time as your gut intuition is something that is often hidden away in a dusty internal cupboard that needs taking out for a good old shine – and like all things, it will need attention and focus.

We're not getting all airy-fairy and cosmic here, although it's a shame that it can be viewed like that in some circles, as gut intuition is a valuable part of the human toolkit.

As Valerie van Mulukom, Research Associate in Psychology says: "Indeed, relying on your intuition generally has a bad reputation, especially in the Western part of the world where analytic thinking has been steadily promoted over the past decades. Gradually, many have come to think that humans have progressed from relying on primitive, magical, and religious thinking to analytic and scientific thinking. As a result, they view emotions and intuition as fallible, even whimsical, tools"

People feel their gut intuition differently: from a blast in the gut itself, to cold shivers, to goosebumps, to feeling you are on the yellow brick road where it all flows smoothly, to picking up clues from the media, or nature, on what path to follow, or to meeting people and listening to what they have to say. We often ask ourselves: Who and what will we meet today that will help us on the journey?"

Chrissie feels her gut intuition often as goosebumps or shivers down her back. Sometimes these can be very strong! At other times, especially when we're being creative, she gets animated and has a sense of something being 'right'.

Livvy says: "It's when there is an excitement and an energy to follow a story, or a person and I have no idea why, but I have to do it - I feel the electricity of it and I have to continue to follow it and it's always been the right thing to do."

It's being brave enough to take the first step to connect with people and – very importantly - asking for what you want. This might feel like you're taking a risk but, ask yourself, what is the worst thing that can happen to you? Okay, so they can reject you, say "no", but you're never on the wrong track – sometimes people might only be with you for a little bit of the journey, not the whole journey, but they will give you something for the next step. That might be the information you need to know to go on a different path.

If you look back in your life you can probably see all the twists and turns that you had to take to end up in the right place. We know it's hard to trust but as we get older, and hopefully a bit wiser, we see we can trust that following our gut intuition always takes us to the right place. Who says that this journey doesn't have its highs and lows, its ups and downs? It's not always a smooth ride… that's where trust comes into play. It is all part of learning some wisdom on this journey called Life.

So, we could say that it's in the bravery of following the electrical current (some might call it a 'buzz') of attraction that will lead us on the first step down the yellow brick road of the new adventure. We cannot see electricity, but we know it is there when the light comes on. We cannot see WIFI, but we know it is there when we connect to the internet. We cannot see our gut intuition, but we can use it just as effectively.

'Six degrees of separation' is the theory that everyone is six or fewer steps away, by way of introduction, from any other person in the world, so that a chain of 'a friend of a friend' statements can be made to connect any two people in a maximum of six steps. This theory was originally proposed by

Connections (Following Your Gut Intuition)

Frigyes Karinthy in 1929, and later popularised by a play of the same name by John Guare in 1990. (Oxford College, Emory).

We always trusted that we would know somebody... who knew somebody... who knew somebody... when we wanted to get a celebrity or other person on the show. We just had to make the first step with the first connection. And sometimes that's all it took! Hence connecting with Jack Oliver, former president of The Beatles Apple Records label... who comes more into the story shortly!

Starting to tell this story felt like looking at a huge basket of multicoloured wool that was in a huge, tangled mess... so many colours... so many threads... but slowly and carefully we got the threads in line so that each ball was in order – that's how we want to begin this story.

The beginning of the connections, the first step along the yellow brick road, starts with our mentor at Radio 2 Helen Thomas who inspired us and fired our imaginations to do a music audio special with lots of musical enhancements, so there we were yet again back on the train working it all out. We decided to do a 'Summers of Love' radio special featuring a load of legendary artists that laid the path to the music of today. These artists of their time were amazing trailblazers - the Beatles, The Byrds, Joni Mitchell, Frank Zappa, Crosby, Stills, Nash and Young, Bob Dylan, Eric Clapton just to name a few. And of course, the music was just fab!

But how to get some relevant interviews? After all, these people aren't exactly easy to connect with... or are they?

Then, randomly, Livvy was posting a tweet from the show and just happened to see a tweet pop up from a man called Jack Oliver... she was intrigued because she liked his hat, read a bit more, and it turned out he happened to be the president of Apple Records from 1969 to 1971. So of course, we tweeted him, he replied... and we ended up interviewing him and hearing all about his amazing journey along the yellow brick road and how he started working with The Beatles!

So here we are another step on the yellow brick road of connections, not quite sure where it's leading, but having trust. In the interview, he gives a great quote that just about sums up what we have been talking about. He says: "It's all about being in the right place at the right time, and then knowing you are there and grabbing the moment!" So, Jack, we think you're right... and glad we were at the right place and right time to meet you!

Things come in leftfield when you least expect them, but you must have an openness to the unexpected happening and then... as Jack Oliver says... grab the moment.

Connections (Following Your Gut Intuition)

Our next step along the yellow brick road happened when Roger McGuinn of The Byrds just happened to be coming to the UK and not only that... performing in Bristol... and we were invited to interview him. Whaaat!! Perfect timing! Of course, we jumped at it and got to hear all his amazing stories and how he had his own version of the yellow brick road which he proceeded to tell us – from the Beatles film A Hard Day's Night inspiring him to create what he was famous for - his jingle-jangle guitar sound; to living in the right place at the right time in Laurel Canyon where Joni Mitchell was a neighbour who happily gave him lyrics for a song he needed; and the great relationships he had with Frank Zappa, George Harrison, Tom Petty, and Bob Dylan. Sounds idyllic, but how did he get there... we reckon he followed his gut intuition.

Mr. Glastonbury Festival himself, Michael Eavis, has been a regular on the show because Livvy lived down the road from him in Somerset, she had had dealings with the festival back in the day and the late Arabella Churchill was a friend, and so it felt easy to connect up with Michael. In one interview he told us how he was inspired to start Glastonbury Festival in 1970 and that it was due to seeing the West Coast bands and artists like The Byrds and Frank Zappa play at the Bath Festival at the Bath and West Showground in Somerset!

Michael could have stayed a farmer and looked after the farm after his father's death, but he followed his excitement and passion and saw an avenue out of farming and into rock 'n roll, and he took the first step the very next morning by calling what was then called the Colston Hall in Bristol and asking a helpful receptionist how to get hold of T Rex – which she told him and the rest is history!

Having written this story, we feel we need to join the circle to get the bigger picture so... here goes! Michael Eavis was inspired to create Glastonbury festival by the West Country American bands, including The Byrds, who just happened to come to the UK and perform up the road from him in Somerset! The Byrds singer Roger McGinn was inspired by going to see a Beatles film to create his famous jingle-jangle sound – and of course, The Beatles were very connected to Jack Oliver, who we connected to via a tweet!

We never knew when we individually met these people, until after we met them and spoke to them, that there was this connection between them running all the way through the show - sends shivers down our spine! Who is writing this story anyway?

Motown seemed to call us to follow the next route of connections. We just followed the yellow brick road and decided we fancied making a 'Motown and Beyond' Special. Yet again, no idea how to pull this off... so how did we get the inside story? Well... as we mentioned we had already met Smokey

Robinson in Cardiff and were keeping in touch with him, and this connection led us to legendary producer and musician Mark Davis. Now this man was THE producer – he produced Marvin Gaye, Diana Ross, Earth, Wind and Fire, the Temptations, Smokey Robinson, Stevie Wonder, Lionel Ritchie, and The Jackson Five, and has over 30 platinum and gold albums. Mark is one of those extraordinary people in the industry who is a gentleman – kind, helpful and gracious. He gave us some great stories and again you can see how his life has been one of following connections, energy, and passion, and of being in the right place at the right time. Oh… and a shedload of talent of course!

Livvy & Chrissie interviewing Roger McGuinn of The Byrds

Livvy and Michael Eavis

Mark Davis, Smokey Robinson and Stevie Wonder (photo courtesy of Mark Davis)

Connections (Following Your Gut Intuition)

Mark Davis and Marvin Gaye (photo courtesy of Mark Davis)

How can you achieve more things in your life and connect with your very own Yellow Brick Road? Here's an exercise to help you get in touch with your gut intuition. This would be useful to do daily until you get the feeling of connection with your gut intuition voice inside.

Exercise 3

So, start by being in the moment; by being really present in the moment.

Find a quiet place.

Follow your breath in and out… in and out… in and out…

Keep your eyes open.

Observe what is outside of you - notice everything. Make yourself look at everything carefully; take in all detail of what you see whether it be a lamp or something in the garden; just look at it - really look at it - until your attention and energy is right in the moment.

Breathe deeply and just start to calm yourself down as you sit in the moment. Now close your eyes as we take a step inward; follow your breathing pattern in and out.

Notice if you breathe more in than out, or if they are even.

Now notice how you feel in your body... what sensations do you have?

Are you comfortable?

Sit very quietly.

Now if you want to know the answer to something, ask yourself the question you want to know. Repeat the question slowly a few times to yourself.

Wait. Just be in the moment, breathing.

If you get an answer immediately - great; if it takes time that's fine too, but you will get an answer.

It might not be today - you might have to do the same practice again tomorrow, but you will get an answer.

When you get your answer, still in this very quiet and calm place, ask yourself the question: "Is this right?"

Wait again. Be patient - it may well be a faint whisper of a voice.

Trust that the answer will come to you.

This is the beginning of learning how to connect up with your gut intuition voice, but it's a daily practice to learn how to do it.

You can listen to this exercise on SoundCloud by scanning the QR code

Chapter 4
We Start with The Mind (Stories we have been told)

We women of a certain age have lived a while now and have met and interacted with all sorts of people. We've probably read a huge number of books, papers and magazines, listened to many radio shows and watched a lot of TV and films and have gained a vast amount of information. So, all in all, we have accumulated many, many stories and myths about who we are and who we should be and by now it's possible that these myths are very deeply ingrained. We have probably gathered way too much baggage and fixed beliefs along the way, which we have never queried. It's just the years we've lived. There are some things we might want to hold on to - however, a lot of how we think and feel and some of our self-beliefs haven't been questioned for decades and now we may want to enquire, question and check if we actually agree with some of our thinking about ourselves and society's view of women of a certain age. We very often don't take the time to actually listen to ourselves.

This is a really important time in our lives to clearly say "actually I don't agree with that story and I want to think differently, more positively, more creatively!" Our mind is this amazing computer and we have the ability to programme it. This means that we have a choice in what we think and what we do, but sometimes we don't even realise that we have this choice. There is a constant interplay that happens between societal conditioning and our thinking about ourselves. Societal conditioning is inherent, we've grown up with it and it permeates our mind with negative beliefs about ourselves without our even realising it in many instances. Our negative thoughts are current but they are broadly based on this accumulated inherent societal conditioning, some new, some old. We may not realise it but we are constantly replaying some of these stories to ourselves and some of them may be having a very negative effect on our confidence, self-esteem and resilience.

This is why attractive and strong role models and positive representation of women of a certain age in the media are so truly important. We all need to see someone like ourselves whom we can admire and aspire to; someone who can help us to challenge and defeat the negative stereotypes that we may have picked up along the way.

Our brain has a negative bias, as proven by John Cacioppo. His research shows that our brains are made to be much more sensitive to negative or bad news and that this negativity makes a bigger impact on our brains than positive information does. This bias can powerfully influence how we operate in the world. For the last couple of million years we have been running on survival thinking. Science says we are pre-disposed to keep using the brain to look for those things that might be going wrong or present a threat to our survival. This is our original state, which has protected us, saved us and kept us alive. Fortunately in this present time most of us do not have to be in survival mode but we are still operating as if we have no choice. It's worth considering at this point if you have a tendency to remember the bad things that have happened to you, more than the good things? Research says that this is how we are programmed, but like any good computer programmer, we can change the settings and create new programs.

We are in control of how we view our life and how we face the fears of change and we can choose to step into the unknown bravely but not stupidly. A useful question at this point might be: how do we stop the mind from this looping and repetition of negative stories about ourselves, how do you say "STOP" to the mind? Do you shout "STOP, STOP!" at it? Does it work? Well to be honest, not really. It takes a lot more attention, determination and focus than that, but the good news is that the negative beliefs and fears that are holding us back can most definitely be identified, challenged and ultimately changed or discarded. People used to say that you can't teach an old dog a new trick but we now know from modern brain science that the brain is plastic. Neuroplasticity, or brain plasticity as it is more commonly called, means that the brain has the ability to adapt and change throughout our lifetime. The human brain is amazing and fully capable of reorganizing itself and forming new connections. This means that we are made for change and even though we may have to work on it change will come and we can learn to see ourselves in a whole new way.

We mentioned earlier that we had written and recorded a music track. It sounds so simple, doesn't it... if only!!! Livvy had been a singer in a band in her twenties, but she had not performed since then. Chrissie was absolutely convinced that if she sang, her voice was so bad that the sky would fall down. Well not quite, but she certainly had never ever thought of herself as one day performing on a music track. Now if you recall Livvy had originally written the track in response to Chrissie's moaning about her period and we had performed it live on air with a fixed backing track. When we decided to actually create a professional record this was a whole brand-new ballgame. However, by using all our media contacts, family and friends, we managed to pull together a recording studio, session musicians and backing singer and even persuaded the uber-talented saxophonist Pee Wee Ellis to attend and perform with us. Pulling all of that together was no mean feat in itself and took our usual mix of determination, persistence and disregard of protocols to achieve it, but, in reality, we were used to pulling the proverbial rabbit out of the hat. It's what we did best. However, recording the track itself was much more challenging and, to be frank, totally terrifying. Livvy, who had a clear idea of how she wanted the track to sound, was suddenly hit by lots of fears and doubts... she hadn't done anything like this since she was in her twenties. She couldn't write musical scores to give to the musicians, so how would she be able to convey her thoughts to the other musicians? Would they take any notice? Would she be able to actually sing anything? Would she even be in tune? And anyway, women of a certain age don't rap or make music tracks, do they? As for Chrissie, she was just convinced that she wasn't meant to be there at all. All of Livvy and Chrissie's negative tapes and stories collected over a lifetime were playing big time. But the desire to do this track, to not buy into who we 'should' be, was bigger than all that fear.

As it happened the track came together in only one day, Livvy conveyed all of her musical ideas successfully to the band and Pee Wee Ellis even complimented her on her ability to "hold a tune". Coming from him that is praise indeed! Chrissie had survived her recording booth moment, much to her surprise and can now add "recording artist" to her repertoire, against all the odds. This all goes to show that you can do anything you want as long as you have a bit of talent, plus a lot of determination and persistence and - just as importantly - you don't ever listen to the negative stories that are looping in your mind about yourself!

We Start with The Mind (Stories we have been told)

Legendary Saxophonist Pee Wee Ellis recording the Hot 'n Bothered track

Livvy & Chrissie and Pee Wee Ellis at the recording studio

Livvy & Chrissie music track 'Hot 'n Bothered' cover

So how can we find out what stories we are telling ourselves? We now know that we have choices and that we can have the desire to do something else and not be pulled back by our limiting stories about ourselves. This exercise will help you to identify and ultimately interrupt those stories replaying over again in your own personal film show and to help you interrupt it where you think it needs changing.

Exercise 4

Get into a comfortable position - lying down is always good. Take three slow deep breaths in and out.

Now... notice what your mind is thinking.

Do you have a familiar story that your mind is telling you? One that repeats over and over again.

One that stops you from expressing yourself, or doing something, or feeling good about yourself right now

Start to see it like a film ...

See the characters...

See the story line...

Start to watch it play out in your mind. You are now the observer of this film.

Now... demand of your mind to stop repeating this story... YOU are the producer and director of this film now... feel the strength and power you have to be able to do this.

Feel your strength getting stronger and stronger as you choose to interrupt the film.

Notice where you interrupt the film.

Now take three more slow deep breaths. Notice how your mind feels and how you feel.

Notice what you thought about and how you interrupted it.

When you are ready open your eyes and write down:

The film title, the storyline and the point at which you interrupted your film, so you know that you can do this at any time you experience endless looping thoughts.

You can listen to this exercise on SoundCloud by scanning the QR code

Chapter 5

Inner confidence (Limitation? What limitation?)

The word 'Confidence' is sometimes thrown around a bit like "Do you want a cup of tea?" as if confidence is just always there, ever-present. It might be for some or at certain times in our lives! But it also might not be. So, what is inner confidence? The dictionary defines confidence as "the feeling or belief that one can have faith in or rely on someone or something". That is how we want to feel about ourselves. It's that feeling when you're not stressed and you're not anxious and you think to yourself: "Yes, I can do this!" You have belief in yourself and your abilities to learn and tackle new things. It might be cooking a great meal and it's a success; baking a cake - and it works; starting a course - and finishing it. It might be writing a song, or standing on a stage; or perhaps running a race - because even if you come last, next time you might come second from last and that's how confidence is built. Because confidence is like building a house – you start on a level piece of ground and build it brick by brick, one step at a time.

The process of building confidence is a double-edged sword though – to become confident you have to go through that which scares or even terrifies you; you then become more confident to do it again next time. It is through this process that we develop that faith and belief in ourselves that creates a feeling of inner confidence. This of course is true at any age and it is a part of the journey of life to take the knocks and bounce back older and wiser. So, in theory, women of a certain age have the potential to own and embody plenty of confidence, as we have been there and done it and we know that we can survive our fears and come back even stronger.

In practice though it seems common for women's confidence to decrease as we grow older, go past child-bearing age, and our bodies start to change. Why is this? If our confidence and feelings of self-worth, attractiveness and usefulness have been built around the 'gaze of men' in a patriarchal society, we have to ask ourselves at what point and at what age do we women start to gaze upon ourselves and feel worthy? Laura Mulvey is a feminist film theorist from Britain who coined the term 'The Male Gaze'. She is most well known for her essay on Visual Pleasure and Narrative Cinema. Her theory examined sexual objectification of women within the media, now known as "the Male Gaze" theory. Mulvey believes women in film are "the bearer of meaning and not the maker of meaning," the suggestion here is that women are being objectified and instead of being in charge of the scene they are placed there to be gazed upon by men. This Hollywood norm of women as objects has an undoubted impact on how we feel in the real world and how the world then treats older women. When we decide to put our gaze upon ourselves, do we feel confident? Do we feel like the beautiful, intelligent, sassy, sexy women that we are? If not, maybe our problem is inside and despite all the programming we have received from society we can now take back our power and change this. When we put our gaze upon ourselves, even though we are often terrified to, then we know what we need to do and what actions we need to take if we don't want to let fear or a lack of confidence hold us back and keep us small and we want to keep moving forward and living our life to the fullest. As the American social activist Maggie Kuhn, who was forced into retirement at the age of sixty-five, said: "Speak your mind, even if your voice shakes."

Our society is not truly valuing women of a certain age as much as youth or older men. This sense of not being appreciated and respected, or viewed as attractive or intelligent, eats away at our confidence and eventually we can start to believe we do not have anything of worth or importance to say, do, or offer anymore, as it may seem that very few people want to listen or take any notice. The message from society is that you are out of the race. Bettie Davis once remarked "Old age ain't no place for sissies" and sissies we are not so let's not allow society to shove us to one side, move over, make some room for us as we have so much collective wisdom and knowledge to offer and it's time to hear our thoughts. People often express surprise if you are still working and not retired by a certain age. They can be amazed if you are training for a new career or going back to education. Some feel people feel they have the right to have a negative opinion if you are dressed fashionably or sexily, or if you are sporty and athletic. There can be a patronising response if you say that you're interested in and good at technology and computing. They might even question why you are not a grandmother. The list of responses to women of a certain age for just living their lives is pretty endless. All of these assumptions about how we should be acting and looking now can be very demoralizing and demeaning. We are being subliminally told to "know our place", which in turn can knock our confidence. Natasha Devon of the Guardian wrote that, "Even the most enlightened people are usually surprised when they begin noticing how often they unconsciously reinforce the notion that a woman's worth is nothing more than the sum of her parts. This is something that can be replicated on social media". We all have a role to play in bringing light to this so it can change.

There is a British game show called Room 101 where celebrities nominate items, people or objects to go into a mythical room when they are disliked or redundant or unwanted. We always say that this is where society likes to place women of a certain age. Our place, according to society, is in Room 101! Well, we never did know our place.

Inner confidence (Limitation? What limitation?)

We once went to interview the celebrities at a big national red carpet event for our radio show. When we got there we very soon realised that, as radio presenters, we were not high up on the pecking order and all the SKY TV, MTV, BBC, ITV, TV presenters and their film crews were allowed on to the red carpet to interview the celebs as they walked down, but we were expected to know our place... which was somewhere at the far back of the room. The message was: "Only celebrities go on the red carpet. And we lot with our big cameras and crew can stand just off the carpet and allow presenters to go on the red carpet and interview them. Know your place, don't break the rules, you are just radio presenters and you can have them when we are finished and that's if you are lucky."

Well, obviously we didn't take any notice of that and in fact we joined the celebs on the red carpet and got chatting to them - much to the annoyance of the camera crews! We got some great interviews with our radio mikes (except one but more on that later in the book). In fact, we first met one of our favorite radio show guests Smokey Robinson there, when Livvy said to him "do you know you're the King of Soul?" and he was very modest, so Livvy repeated it twice until he acknowledged it. It was the first of many interviews we did with him and it must have been memorable for him as well, as we found out from his secretary that he had our picture on his office wall that was taken of us all that day. Look, we knew we were breaking all the rules and we were certainly not cut off emotionally from our terror, but we still did it anyway. We are certainly not women who like to be put in our place, especially if the rules don't make any sense to us and of course we wanted to get the interviews. It obviously helped that there were two of us, as we always egg each other on, but we all need to learn to be sassy and confident enough to say: "I'm here and I have something of value to offer. I can do this!"

Livvy & Chrissie with Smokey Robinson

Livvy & Chrissie and The Jacksons

So try this exercise to help you to get in touch with your inner strength and confidence, if you need it, so that if a time comes when you are 'put in your place', or made to feel 'less than' you can decide not to play along as well.

Exercise 5

Sit up on a chair, or on the floor - whatever is most comfortable for you.

Take three deep breaths... in... and out... in... and out... in... and gently out.

Now... allow yourself to find three things that you are frightened of achieving in your life right now... no matter how big or small.

Take a moment to deepen and calm your breathing. See yourself holding a sword in your right hand. This is the sword of confidence, strong and powerful. See its beauty and strength. Feel its full power.

It is formidable.

See what it looks like. It may be encrusted with jewels at its hilt, or plain with shining metal.

Grasp it firmly.

Feel the warrior woman energy searing through

your body... the strong and powerful woman who has the strength and ferocity to face her fears and deal with them.

See yourself wielding it with strength and precision. Use your sword of confidence to slice through your fears to reach the very heart of them... because hidden deep within each fear is your next step.

As you slice through each fear, make a mental note of:

What your fear is...

How is fear stopping you from achieving your goal...?

What is the next step that is hidden deep within that fear...?

Now take three deep breaths in and out...

When you are ready, open your eyes and write down your fears and your plan of action for each one.

Draw a picture of your sword or make a model.

Know you can access your sword of confidence and access your warrior woman energy at any time you need it, so that you can feel confident to achieve anything you want to achieve.

Inner confidence (Limitation? What limitation?)

You can listen to this exercise on SoundCloud by scanning the QR code

Chapter 6
Let's Talk About Money

We asked this question to ourselves and now we're asking you – why is money such a taboo subject? We felt the need to ask this question because we've found that, in some social situations, the subject of money is actively avoided and even considered very 'bad form' to talk about or even mention whatsoever. Livvy moved to live in a small village in the countryside and often there were these 'dinner parties' organized by the local people. She soon found out that you couldn't talk about money, sex or politics at these occasions and so after a while she would run out of things to say. Obviously, that was all she wanted to talk about! She couldn't understand why this was… and thought maybe it was because she was from London… or maybe it was the creative circles she usually moved in where money, sex and politics were commonly spoken about. Anyway, we all know that it's not uncommon for the subject of money to be avoided at all cost!

The thing is… it's really quite new and recent in our history for most women to be financially independent, in fact it is only in the last one hundred and twenty five or so years that women have emerged from the home and into modern industries where they are earning their own money.

It is hard to imagine that as recently as 1975 a married woman could not even get her own credit card unless she had permission from her husband and even if you were single, financial independence was not much easier to attain. So with the relatively recent history we women have had around money and are still having, we still have a huge learning curve compared to men in becoming fully financially empowered. In a large number of ways we have become empowered practically, as lots of women now own their own money and have careers, but we still have a way to go emotionally to get up to speed – there is still an emotional pull to lean on men, financially, or to not be the 'main breadwinner'; or to feel something is amiss or out of place if you are earning more than your partner. We can be every bit as determined as men to earn money and to be financially independent but maybe in a more female way? We don't have to emulate men to be empowered financially, but yes we can learn from them, but then do it in our own sweet way. Helaine Olen, author of Pound Foolish: Exposing the Dark Side of the Personal Finance Industry, says that "women are often told that they need more help or different advice about how to manage their money—just look at the books and websites marketed specifically to women, like Citibank's Women & Co. and Prudential's Women & Money. But the truth is, studies show little difference between women and men's financial knowledge and habits". She looks at the myths that surround women and money only to discover that myths are exactly what they are and the only gap that needs filling is for us women to know that we are as capable as men in every aspect financially.

Let's look at the emotions surrounding the topic of money. Have you ever been in a shop and had your bank card denied... what emotions come up for you? When that has happened to Livvy her first response is "It must be the machine... I know there's money in that account". Chrissie always says "Oh no, I must have forgotten to transfer some money over to that account!" But what we're really saying is that it seems to cause embarrassment... and I think that most of us would admit to feeling embarrassed in this situation. So why is that? Why should we be embarrassed at all? It is clear that money affects us more deeply than the size of our bank balance. There's a lot of fear, shame and anger and it seems these are common emotions that surround money. What does it feel like when you realise you're down to your last pound? And what does it feel like when you've got thousands in the bank?

These questions are the beginning of the quest to finding out the difference between money as the 'object' and money as the 'emotion'. A lot of us have great fantasies about winning the lottery - on the one hand we imagine the freedom to do what we really want to do and on the other hand we would like to have the status and the power... which, if it happens, can lead to arrogance and actually, ultimately, it's just money. Unfortunately, in our society some people have more respect for wealthy people and you are treated in a superior way if you are considered well off. So this behavior supports us to have these emotional reactions to having more or less amounts of money as we expect people to treat us differently based on this and we all know how much us humans like to feel accepted and respected. The truth is that the problem is not money – the problem is how we approach money... think about money... and how we handle money in every respect.

Jonathon Swift wrote that: "A wise person should have money in their heads and not in their hearts". So in the spirit of all things Livvy and Chrissie... here is a story of how not to behave around money! We were driving home from an interview in the city centre and there was a major hold up all over the city, all the roads were blocked and we were late for our next interview. So... egged on by Livvy, Chrissie decided to take a quick short cut... that turned out to be up a small one-way street, going the wrong way ("I swear, m'lord, it was an honest mistake"). Unfortunately, in her hurry she accidentally whacked off a parked cars' wing mirror! Of course, she screeched to a halt and we both looked in horror at the damaged mirror as it hung on a few wires now dangling in the wind... then as if by magic the owner of the car arrived! There was lots of "I'm terribly sorry – it was an accident" whilst the cars coming in the correct direction hooted at us to move. But the owner was a lovely guy and a deal was made: £50 job done. So Livvy got the said money and gave it to him. There was relief all round! Chrissie then proceeded to back up the one-way street and as we got to the top and drove hurriedly away, Livvy asked "how do we know it was his car?" We looked at each other and realised we had no idea and we still don't to this very day.

Seriously though, research shows that as we now live longer than ever before with the average female lifespan being 81 years compared to 1990 where it was just 67.7 years, that is a very big jump in just in a mere 20 years. There are a lot of women who, through no fault of their own, end up alone – perhaps because of illness, bereavement, divorce or separation – and suddenly find themselves ill-equipped to deal with their new and often challenging financial situation. Not only are they learning to cope alone, they're also learning how to manage financially alone. So we believe it is really, really important to get to grips with all the ins and outs of money as early in life as possible. Ideally this should be on the curriculum in schools, teaching children how to deal with money throughout their lives.

When we interviewed the legendary Roger McGuinn of the Byrds for the first time, we asked him what advice he would give to young, aspiring musicians nowadays. We expected perhaps a reply emphasizing persistence or creativity but no – he was very, very emphatic about how they needed to really get the contractual side of things sorted out first – the percentage of money that goes to themselves; the song rights; and the management and agency deals – something often musicians and other artistic souls aren't that savvy about, leaving them open to much exploitation. It takes a lot to be famous – take Taylor Swift; she is a well-known artist but she lost the rights to the masters of her first six albums, therefore losing a lot of money.

So back to us, oh women of a certain age. Are we in charge of our lives, financially speaking? Are we aware of any pitfalls lurking in the shadows, or conversely, any opportunities that may lie ahead? And if not, why not? Whether you are single, married, dating, working or not working, well off or not so well off, it is important to get to grips with it. When we interviewed the Rt. Hon Harriet Harman MP a few years ago regarding her Commission on Older Women, one of the things she told us was that unemployment amongst women of a certain age had increased by forty one per cent in the last two and a half years, compared with one per cent overall and that the pay gap between women and men over age fifty was twice as large as for women overall. It seems from these figures that nothing much has changed. One of our more famous 'coups' as we like to call them, was about banknotes! We once interviewed Ed Miliband, MP, the then Leader of the Opposition and he was talking about how we needed more women on banknotes. So Livvy asked him (well, she was well prepared): "If you need more women on banknotes, what about Chrissie and ME?" He said he'd ask the Governor of the Bank of England and that we were definitely on the short list! If you can't spend it, at least be on it, we thought.

So now, let's move on from humour to the psychology of money. Olivia Mellan, an American author, therapist and consultant and a leader in the field of money psychology, says that "for most people, money is never just money; it is a tool to accomplish some of life's goals. It is love, power, happiness, security, control, dependency, independence, freedom and more. Money is so loaded a symbol that to unload it and I believe it must be unloaded to live in a fully rational and balanced relationship to money that reaches deep into the human psyche. Usually, when the button of money is pressed, deeper issues emerge that have long been neglected. As a result, money matters are a perfect vehicle for awareness and growth." That can all sounds a bit daunting, especially when all you are trying to do is to make ends meet. But it's well worth taking some time to think about what feelings money, or more specifically, talking honestly about your financial situation, brings up for you.

Livvy & Chrissie and Harriet Harman

Here's an exercise to help you see what emotions you may have around money.

We recommend that you take at least 15 minutes for this exercise, so the deeper messages have a chance to be heard.

Exercise 6

Here are three questions for you to consider. Really take your time to think about each one and write down your answers.

1) What is my relationship with money?

Do you like it...?

Don't want to think about it...?

Do you measure your status by it...? Or lack of status by it...?

Is it your friend...?

Is it just something for transaction...?

Is it an energy...?

2) What have I been told about money?

Write a list of what you've been told.

Who told you – was this from family, friends, society?

See if you can remember and write the statements you were told about money. See if you agree with them or not.

3) What do I need to do differently from now on in relation to money to make it work better for me?

Be conscious of the money coming in and the money going out. Write down all your daily transactions. You can do this with a notebook or put it on your phone. If you start to feel anxious, find out why.

Are you unnecessarily over-cautious with money?

This is the time to really have a good look at your relationship with money.

You can listen to this exercise on SoundCloud by scanning the QR code

Chapter 7
Loving your Body Changes

It is so easy to write the words 'loving your body changes' about the wrinkles... the menopause... the sagging boobs and dropping bums! In reality, loving our body changes can be extremely hard and even painful. How do we learn to look at ourselves in the mirror and go: "Okay, my body's changed - and is changing - but I'm doing well". What are we saying to ourselves daily as we look in the mirror? The external body police tell us to "stay youthful, younger is better and slim is better, tight skin is better than loose skin" and on and on it goes. If you are listening and if you are internalizing those messages and agreeing with them it becomes a dark, defeating hole. So, no – we are not going there! We refuse to.

As the journalist Suzanne Moore has written: "If you measure your worth by how you look now, without appreciating the beauty you have become as you age, you are in trouble." But when you grow older in a society that only values youthful beauty, with nothing sagging, nothing deteriorating or ageing, then it can be extremely hard to come to terms with your bodies many changes as you age. There may be a sense of loss and a period of grief to go through as you come to terms with what is happening. So how can we turn all of this on its head and not put such focus on the deteriorating body, but instead accept the changes, love the changes and even learn to move freely with the energy of these changes? We have to dig deep within ourselves, behind the conditioning, stereotypes and myths, to access our non-age archetypal images of ourselves - because when we do, we will feel into and shape the power of our innate creative energy and that is what will allow us to see our bodies in a completely different light.

The psychoanalyst Carl Jung says that there are seven different female archetypes which are described as powerful universal symbols that if pointed out to us, we can all recognise as very familiar to us. We have been drip-fed these archetypes throughout our lives beginning at a very young age through fairy stories, films, books and TV shows. The seven female Jungian archetypes are the Maiden, the Queen, the Lover, the Mother, the Huntress, the Sage and the Mystic. Each one of these has its own power, characteristics and energetic force that we can access and use at different times throughout our lives, although we may each have personally had one or more dominant ones throughout our lives.

Why is it so useful for us to have some understanding of the archetypes that are within all of us? We believe it's because it gives us some choice of not just reacting, but to be able to clearly choose to be a certain way in the world, to take some emotional control over our lives and to know when we are reacting and being propelled by others views of us. It is through knowing ourselves more deeply that we can gain a confidence and a surety in our lives. Knowing that each of us has inside of us such attributes as strength, confidence, playfulness, joy, happiness and wisdom and that all we have to do is tap into them, sounds so very easy - and in a way it is! We have been fed many fairy stories throughout our lives, from a very young age, after which we move onto films, books and TV shows continuously reinforcing these archetypes in our subconscious mind. All of the archetypes are represented clearly to us there. To put it in simple terms: the good person (Snow White), the bad person (Voldemort in the Harry Potter books), the seductress (Actress Elizabeth Taylor), the sweet one (Doris Day), the clever one (Amal Clooney), the spiritual one (The Dalai Lama), the flaky one (Phoebe in Friends) etc. So we know them all very well and can sometimes identify with these archetypes and see them in people that we know.

The cutting-edge TV show 'Sex and the City' was the first of its kind to allow the sexuality of four women to be portrayed in a normal everyday way. The four women in the series each portrayed a classic female archetype. Take Samantha for example - she was definitely the huntress and also the lover archetype. These archetypes form the basis of much of our instinctive behavior, so it's really useful for us to start to learn about them, certainly for women of a certain age, because we can use them as a template for ageing well. Archetypes are like a deep reservoir of our human experience; we all have them within us and they are activated all the time by different things such as other people, nature or the media. Anything that happens outside of ourselves will call into play our archetypes. However, when we understand the archetype, we can then choose to activate the one we wish or need to use at that time.

The one we are going to focus on for accepting our bodies is the Lover archetype and we're going to reclaim it with huge passion. The Lover is the oldest feminine archetype and when this energy is active in our psyche, our energy field is charged, we are vibrant and alive and we become a magnet to those around us. We can feel a charisma and passion surge through our body that is truly ageless. All women have direct access to this Lover archetypal energy. If we can connect with this archetypal energy and use its charismatic and creative energy, we start to experience it as the powerful driving force that it is in our lives. Then we will start to love our bodies as they are right now, as we will be endowed with a new vitality, charm and charisma, which in turn makes us feel beautiful and attractive, inside and out. We can then walk in the world feeling sensual beautiful and desirable. We will get that mirror reflection from the world saying "Yes!" back to us. Mirroring or limbic synchrony as it is also known is a very real phenomenon. Carol

Kinsey Gorman says that "In human beings, it was found that mirror neurons not only simulate actions, they also reflect intentions and feelings. As such, they play a key role in our ability to socialize and empathize with others". Mirroring occurs on an unconscious level when one person imitates the speech patterns, movement and attitude of the other person. Although we are usually not aware of it this happens all the time in social situations, especially with family members and close friends. Without knowing it we are replicating another person's nonverbal signals to us. Knowing this can make us more aware of what signals we are actually sending out to be reflected back to us and we can use this awareness to enhance our own lives. Think of Latino women and Afro Caribbean women, Italian women, especially women of a certain age - curvaceous, walking tall, strutting even, as they go about their business. They exude great inner confidence and they are ageing magnificently! This in turn is what the world will mirror back to them.

Talking of charisma, the exceptionally charming and very funny actor Anthony Head and his wife Sarah, an animal behavior expert, were often guests on our show and we have had many absolutely hilarious moments with them over the years. Livvy would sometimes be laughing so hard that she could barely present the show. One regular feature we did was that we used to find funny or quirky headlines to comment on with our guests and on one memorable occasion, the headline was about whether there should be a more realistic larger sized Barbie doll to properly represent the true female shape, to which Tony replied "How about a pot-bellied Ken then?" Unsurprisingly we all fell about laughing but funnily enough, Matell did actually bring out a pot-bellied, balding Ken doll shortly after that! It made us think we definitely need to have an older Barbie in production. Young girls and all women need to be prepared that it is normal and natural to age and it can also be really beautiful.

As the wonderful Eartha Kitt once said "Ageing has a wonderful beauty and we should have respect for that." As women we can often look forward and see our life ahead as the burden of more wrinkles and more bits going southwards but yet why focus on what we don't have? Why not focus on the body we can have... sensuous, energised, healthy, vital, alive and still beautiful.

Livvy & Chrissie with Tony Head and Sarah Fisher

Livvy & Chrissie and Anthony Head

Here is an exercise to help you get access to your inner creative energy. When we connect with our creative energy, it endows us with a powerful charisma and an attractive energy and passion and you will feel and look beautiful whatever your body shape or size.

Exercise 7

Lie down somewhere comfortable and take three deep breaths... one in... and out... one in... and out... one in... and gently out.

Sink deeper and deeper into your relaxation as you journey down into the place where you feel your creative lover energy arising... a potent, primordial force that drives you onwards and gives you energy life and charisma.

Allow yourself to fully experience the deep creative urge that all of us women have...

Feel yourself surrender to its power and vigour...

You now notice a door ahead of you... a beautiful carved door that entices you to enter...

Allow yourself to enter...

You find yourself in a room... a huge beautiful, sensuous room filled with so many colours... textures... shapes... materials... gorgeous objects... beautiful plants... a room of your own design...

Everything you could possibly think of to be your true creative self with is in this room...

The air is literally pulsating with energy...

You walk around the room... it seems to have no limits to its size. You admire everything... and everything is stunningly beautiful... sensual... seductive.

You find yourself drawn to certain colours... objects... crafts... tools... materials...

You now realise you have a passionate creative desire growing inside of you and a deep appreciation of the body you have right now.

Feel the power... passion... and joy of it...

Allow it to surge through you touching every cell in your body until you are consumed with creative energy...

Slowly notice your breathing... and follow the breath in and out... let yourself slowly come back to the room...

Open your eyes and when you are ready, take some time to write down how you accessed this energy...

What object did see that will remind you of this deep appreciation of your body?

Look at it daily.

You can listen to this exercise on SoundCloud by scanning the QR code

Chapter 8
Hot 'n Bothered (Menopause)

We decided to tackle this emotive subject because we noticed that there is so much negativity about it out there and we felt it really needed addressing in a more positive and hopeful light. Firstly, menopause is a brand new chapter in our lives. So, it begs the question… how do we feel about this change in our own lives generally? Maybe we don't like change and respond to it with fear and trepidation, not fully seeing or appreciating how amazing it can be. As humans we are made to fear newness because it is associated with uncertainty. But research has shown that when people feel competent about the change that is ahead (back to our confidence again) they will accept change more easily. Oprah Winfrey said: "So many women I've talked to see menopause as an ending. But I've discovered this is your moment to reinvent yourself after years of focusing on the needs of everyone else. It's your opportunity to get clear about what matters to you and then to pursue that with all of your energy, time and talent.".

This is why we feel it is very important and in fact vital to talk about the menopause and what can be done to make this transition easier for women. Wasn't it said that a journey of a thousand miles must begin with a single step? So… let's go back to your very first period. Do you remember your first period – the mess and the chaos? Maybe you remember the fear or the confusion? It is the first major change that we as women have to come to terms with in our bodies, as well as growing breasts and body hair. After that comes the constant waiting every month for mood swings and body reactions and always, always having to be prepared. Then comes the incessant fears of pregnancy: the "Am I...? Aren't I...?" It is really never-ending.

A very powerful film that came out in the 1960's was called Cathy Come Home, written by Ken Loach. It managed to expose what a lot of women knew sadly all too well already... the shame, desperation and dire consequences of getting pregnant 'out of wedlock'. We actually interviewed Ken Loach recently, after another one of his social commentary films, 'I, Daniel Blake' came out. We had to let him know that the film 'Cathy Come Home' was pivotal for women at that time, to take the stigma away from being a single mother, to not feel ashamed and to allow single mums to hold their heads up high like all mothers should be able to do. It is almost hard to imagine in this day and age what it was like back then. He must be saluted for this and It was most definitely an honour to interview him.

So... back to our journey. The next phase, if you are wanting a child, is all the "Am I...? Aren't I...? Can I...? Can't I...?" that goes with the territory each month and of course the sheer joy and delight when you find out you are, or the heartache when you are not. If you do not want a child, then the feeling is utter despair if that test shows positive and also relief when it doesn't. Stressful or what! Soooo... then we come to no more periods... we are in the Menopause! Hot... sticky... not sleeping... tired... reacting. This, however, is now seen as a 'Bad Thing', not as that we are in the middle of a change, it is not seen as that we can take control - this is just a 'Bad' experience to be both suffered and endured. This view of the menopause is creating a lot of fear and trepidation for women who haven't even reached the menopause yet – it's like telling a bad birth story to a pregnant woman – why do it? We decided to move away from the 'Coven of the Menopausal Women', as we call it, where it's all about the suffering and there is seemingly no hope and nothing is said about how this is natural and all a part of our body changing and that of course we can take control and do something about it. Whether you have lots of money or little money, it is possible to get help, as we have found out on our own personal journeys.

Livvy's menopausal journey consisted of a lot of hot flushes that went on for a few weeks, before she then went to see an acupuncturist, which seemed to completely get rid of them; however, within that month she found an exhaustion in her that was what she calls 'grey tiredness'. From her place on the floor she hunted and researched and talked to many women and found out about Dr Hertoghe in Belgium, a world-famous doctor who specializes in bio-identical hormones. Three months later her energy levels were back - and even more so! Dr Hertoghe says that our hormones decrease from the age of 30 years old and onwards and especially if you have had children, so that by the time you hit your 50s you are in trouble. His thinking is that we need to balance our hormones from the age of 30 onwards, so we don't have to suffer in this way. Often though, women come to him in the middle of menopause, rather than as a preventative measure for a less extreme transition.

Chrissie was lucky enough to have a doctor that was willing to help her with her early signs of hormonal imbalance which began in her forties. She was working full-time, still having periods but noticed that she was struggling with her tiredness a lot more. She had already started on additional hormones before the menopause, then she joined Livvy and started seeing De Hertoghe and the rest as they say is history. Speaking of Dr Hertoghe, the first time we went to his offices in Belgium, it was a bit like walking back into a sixties film! The walls were bright orange, purple, yellow, lime green, you name a colour and it was on the wall. And the plastic chairs were bright neon as well. Well, take what you like and leave the rest, we thought! We interviewed him and he was very charming and knowledgeable and it was really a great relief to find someone who actually knew – and cared – so much about women's hormones. So... of course we had to try them. This is in Brussels and we were sent to the nearby chemist to get all the necessary medication that the doctor had prescribed. Yes, they stock this stuff! Yes, it's considered normal to look after yourself in this way! Well, we filled our hand luggage with our potions and lotions, gels and pills, so full to the top; we could hardly close our cases. Then off to the airport we went and now this is where things all got a bit 'Sex in the City'. After our hand luggage had passed through a security check, the customs man pulled us both aside, emptied our cases and checked each and every pot – slightly embarrassing to say the least, we felt like we were drug barons – then they saw our covering letters... and eventually we were let through. Now at this point we were late for our flight and we could hear it being announced on the tannoy. Cue women of a certain age frantically dashing through the airport through miles of corridor – because, of course, our gate was right at the other end of the airport. We just barely made it in time, absolutely hot 'n bothered (this wasn't menopause – this was just two unfit women running!) and then as Livvy tries to put her bag in the above locker, this chap, who it transpires has a lot of film equipment, tells her that his equipment was more important that her drugs and that she should put her bag in the hold to make room for it. Let's just say it was a perfect cue for a potential meltdown but, ten out of ten, she totally held it together, raised herself up to as tall as she could be, looked him directly in the eye and said, with feeling: "you must be having a laugh". He swiftly backed down. The long and short of it was, we got it all home eventually and have never felt better!

Now you know there is life after the menopause: we are all so busy looking at the suffering of the menopause that we are not looking at what comes next. Well the good news is that it's like entering the Garden of Eden. Sex can be amazing, there is no fear of pregnancy, hormones are zinging and there is a freedom that you don't realise you have, until you've got through this gateway. You are not ruled by monthly suffering, food cravings or fear of pregnancy – not to mention all that endless contraception! All tension is gone from your body. Mother Nature stops screaming: "Have another baby, have another baby." It is unthinkable up until this point, to realise how much stress was carried in our bodies all of those years, how much pressure to conceive or not conceive and your body becomes just yours now, to enjoy in a completely stress-free way. So, there is hope and there is a very good reason for going through this passage of the menopause; it's important to hold this in mind while you go through it - that this is a journey... and that there is another story about to unfold.

As journalists we have researched all the available options - and although we are not 'born again' about it - we did want to share with you what we have found out along the way, which may or may not be what you want to do, of course. We now have a documentary in mind to raise awareness and share with women what is available in the UK to help to make the transition through the menopause easier, so that women from all walks of life can get help, if they so choose. We interviewed a consultant, Dr. Annie Evans, in Bristol, UK, who specialized in female issues and she told us how many women come to her in desperation, they have often even been prescribed anti-depressants for menopausal issues. We also interviewed consultant Mrs. Caroline Overton and she confirmed with us that, after an initial consultation where she will do a full assessment and give her expert opinion on what hormones you may need, she will write a letter of recommendation to your doctor so that you can get your GP to give you a prescription for body-identical hormones. This means that you can now get these hormones on the NHS in the UK – which means that if money is tight, these hormones are free or available for the cost of a prescription – amazing or what!

We want to point out that bio-identical hormones are very precisely chosen to go with your body and your deficiencies. We've come a very long way, regarding menopause… and there still is a long way to go. But you know this could be an amazing ride - and we look forward to meeting you on the other side, if you haven't already arrived yet. Here is an exercise to help you on your journey.

Exercise 8

Lie somewhere comfortable, where you won't be disturbed for a while.

Take several deep slow breaths... in... out... in... out...

Let your breathing deepen...

Imagine you are walking along a beautiful forest path under a green and golden canopy of dappled light...

As you slowly walk further along the path, you come to a clearing...

In front of you is a marvellous ancient stone entrance... the stones are covered in soft green lichen... the ground is covered with fresh pine needles and smells so fragrant...

You realise that it is the entrance to a cave... you take a deep breath and slowly enter...

The walls of the cave are made of stone... you can see them glistening... it is warm and inviting...

As you go further into the cave you feel a sense of wonder and anticipation...

And as you go even further you see at the end of the cave... a beautiful old woman... she is in a wooden rocking chair... she exudes joy... wisdom... and beauty...

In front of her is a stool covered with a soft blanket... she wants you to sit there...

You realise that she is the wisdom of all women and knows the passage of time...

You tell her your hopes and fears about your body ageing... and she tells you a message purely for you, on how to be in this next chapter of your life...

You sit together in peace and silence as the message sinks in... There is a feeling of calmness and serenity as you sit in this beautiful cave together...

Then it is time to go... you thank her and slowly make your way out through the cave covered in pine needles... out through the lichen-covered stone entrance... and back into the sunlight and into the forest...

Take some deep breaths... let the sun warm you up and caress you...

Slowly walk back through the forest...

Now take a big, deep breath... and another... and another.

Slowly allow your eyes to open...

When you are ready, write down what you learnt.

You can listen to this exercise on SoundCloud by scanning the QR code

Chapter 9

Fashion or Style (Projecting what you wish out into the world)

Fashion should be about dressing how we feel and only to please only ourselves. It is about wearing what makes us feel happy, wearing what makes us feel good, what colours we love and what styles we like. It's also a way of expressing who we wish to be today and what we wish to express. There is no correct way to dress. Obviously, we have formulaic styles such as casual, smart, party, fun, work, formal etc., but within all of that, gone are the days where we are having to follow such defined rules of how to look and what to wear in order to be acceptable. No judgment, no moral high ground. No "it's superficial" and we don't need it. It's okay to love fashion and to be a deep and meaningful person too. It's okay to want to change the world and to still look fabulous and feel amazing. Designer Vivienne Westwood once said: "Fashion is very important. It is life-enhancing and, like everything that gives pleasure, it is worth doing well" We want to be seen as having our own unique style – one that we discovered and molded for ourselves. You're never too old to go for wearing what makes you feel happy, sexy, or free, and dressing for ourselves because it makes us feel good is the very best way to do it. Do we dress for ourselves, do we dress for other women, or do we dress for men? This is a question worth asking ourselves every day. The clothes we wear define us and allow us to express our inner and our outer, selves.

After all, if it wasn't for the fashion designer Coco Chanel, one of the 100 most influential women in our history, we might still all be wearing corsets! She saw women being unable to breathe properly in the restrictive fashion dictates of the time and went and decided to change it. She has also given the world some iconic clothing, from chic and practical trousers for women to the little black dress... the LBD! She famously said, "You live but once; you might as well be amusing." We like her style. The thing to remember is that your own personal style never goes out of fashion. Style isn't fashion - style is about expressing yourself in a way that makes you feel good and authentic while also letting people know the sort of person you are and how you wish the world to perceive you. Clothes can make us less invisible in the world (unless of course we choose to be). As Anna Wintour said, "Just be true to yourself and listen as much as one is able to other people whose opinions you respect and look up to but in the end it has to come from you".

At work, before we ever wrote a script, or learned what it was we were presenting, Livvy would always make the enquiry: "What's the image... what are we wearing... how do we complement each other... what sort of colours?" It was clothes first, then the

Fashion or Style (Projecting what you wish out into the world)

script for presenting next. It was like if we put on the correct look, the words would just flow. Style is having the confidence to wear what we love and not wear something because it's been dictated to you from external sources, or is allegedly age-appropriate. What is this age appropriateness anyway? Who dictated it? That's something that has really puzzled us both. Where and when was it decided that we had to look a certain way over the age of 45? How did this happen? Maybe if we had parents or grandparents who were conservative in their dress code, we felt we had to follow suit. Maybe it's the magazines and TV shows - or that look you are given by someone as if you have a bad smell. Maybe we have also felt that we have had to diminish our sexuality and sensuality in the way we dress because we are subliminally told that it isn't 'appropriate' for a woman of a certain age to be sexy! We are talking about the confidence that clothes, fashion and your personal style bring to you... and why not? It's having the confidence to wear something that, when you look in the mirror, makes you think: "I look great! I feel good!" not only when you are looking for a relationship or going for a job interview but whenever you just feel like it. How about instead we think about fashion like a piece of art, you are starting with a blank canvas – you - and the clothes that you are going to wear are like a paint box. Fashion and style say: "we are not invisible, we like colour, we like fabrics and we want to look good and feel good."

You have to be discerning and know what suits you – not what fashion dictates. One season it was: 'Wear yellow! Or Citrus green, with a horizontal striped tee-shirt' and we thought: "You must be having a laugh – those colours make us look ill and being women of boobs wearing a horizontal striped tee-shirt – you must be joking!" You have to find what you love, what your style is and what suits you best. Ask a friend, be brave and, if on the first go it looks wrong on you, it's definitely wrong! And don't be persuaded otherwise. You must feel good in what you are wearing to allow your inner light to shine outwards.

Mark Heyes, the fashion designer and TV presenter, came up with some brilliant ideas for us when he has been on the show, but there was one time when he suggested to Livvy that she would look great in a beany hat and this suggestion was met with a horrified response of: "Absolutely not! It would make my head look like a peanut! And I'm a Trilby girl." We all fell about laughing of course and he wasn't at all offended that Livvy didn't like his suggestion. Now that's a true professional. Another time at the big media event we mentioned earlier, when we interviewed the celebrities on the red carpet we had an interesting encounter with the rap superstar Neo. Being women of a certain age and talking to The Jacksons, Smokey, Fern Cotton and all, neither of us actually realised who he was. If that wasn't embarrassing enough, he actually came up to us and asked if we wanted to interview him.

Well, not wishing to be rude, Livvy started asking him about his stunning red leather Chanel jacket, which started off: "Oh my God, where did you get your jacket? I absolutely love your jacket!", to which he replied "Chanel", and they ended up having a really good conversation about fashion and style. So the bonding was there but we still didn't know who he was though, until Chrissie's teenage son was completely horrified later on when she told him the story. This story just goes to show that fashion is always a great conversation starter, it can denote a shared love of clothes and also demonstrate being part of the same gang - although of course we couldn't afford a Chanel jacket like that, maybe we can find a similar one at a quarter of the price!

We have noticed when we are out and about that one or the other of us will often talk to people – mostly women – about what they are wearing. From the supermarket to the red carpet, talking clothes with strangers opens up friendships, allows connections to be made and offers a good happy moment for all.

Livvy & Fashionista Mark Heyes and Andrew Barton Celebrity Hairdresser

Livvy & Chrissie Fashionista Mark Heyes and Andrew Barton Celebrity Hairdresser

Fashion or Style (Projecting what you wish out into the world)

Livvy & Chrissie with Fashionistas Henry Holland and Mark Heyes

Livvy with Jeanne Marine and Jerry Hall

Livvy Fashionista moment

Try this exercise to find or reclaim your true fashion style.

Exercise 9

Lie down somewhere comfortable.

Take three deep breaths... one in... one out... one in... one out... one in... one out...

Allow yourself to relax deeply.

Fashion or Style (Projecting what you wish out into the world)

Now... remember the first outfit you wore as a child.

What does it look like?

What colours? What shapes?

Now... remember an outfit you wore at aged around 15 years old.

What does it look like?

What colours? What shapes?

What length? What style?

Now... remember what you wore aged around 20 years old.

What does it look like?

What colours... shape... materials... style?

How did you feel as you were out and about wearing it?

Allow yourself to remember.

Now... take three deep breaths... in... and out... and slowly come back to the present.

Bring with you the colours and shapes you loved... and enjoyed moving in.

Open your eyes and make a note of them so you don't forget the joy of dressing up.

See how you can bring them into your image now.

Write down the different outfits you remembered.

Write down how you might want to make changes to the clothes you wear now.

Draw pictures of them if you like.

Experiment with wearing different accessories and colours.

If you can, go to a store with a trusted and honest friend and try some outfits on that reflect these changes.

Reflect on how they make you feel.

You can listen to this exercise on SoundCloud by scanning the QR code

Chapter 10
Make Up and Image (Enhancing what you already have)

We obviously had to talk about makeup, which has a very long and interesting history. Cosmetic body art is argued to have been the earliest form of ritual in our human culture. It seems that women throughout the ages have always wanted to enhance their beauty. From 10,000BC in Ancient Egypt and 3,300BC in Southern Europe, people started tattooing their skin and also wearing eye make-up and lip enhancers such as certain berries to redden their lips. The Ancient Egyptians are well known for their women wearing make-up (think Elizabeth Taylor in Cleopatra!). It was actually the ancient Egyptians who regarded beauty as a sign of holiness that in around 4000 BC invented eye make-up. Many cultures, such as the Ancient Greeks, did not want their women to be seen as desirable and wanted them in the home, so we can guess from this that they didn't like their wives wearing make-up. In other cultures, make-up was often used to show tribal allegiance and to scare the opposition. In many cultures decoration of the self was considered immoral, or viewed as going against 'traditional' or 'respectable' values. Make-up also had very strong religious connotations throughout history. Early Christian writers created a powerful association between make-up and deception and that same underlying, subliminal message has continued to be an issue for us women, as if wearing make-up is wrong or bad. Why should we feel we are not being ourselves if we wear make-up? Who do we become when wearing some blusher, lippy and mascara? Do we become this deceptive woman that we are so often portrayed to become? We think not.

During the early 1900s make-up was still not excessively popular and could not yet be bought in department stores. However, it became fashionable in the United States and Europe from 1910 onwards, due to the popularity of ballet, theatre and films; people like Max Factor opened a salon (yes, he was a real person!) and the rest is history. It's a worthwhile thought that maybe we are still wearing make-up – lippy, nail polish, eye-liner, defined eyebrows etc. – to show our female tribal allegiance, to be part of a female gang. The question remains though: are we meant to leave the tribe at a certain age? Is it only a youth tribe that has a sell-by date? Instead of the idea that make-up is only for the young, we think that perhaps it is for all of us, at any age, to help us be the best and most beautiful we can be and to enhance ourselves – for ourselves.

As the American businesswoman and fashionista Sophia Amoruso once commented: "When I put on make-up, I'm not doing it to pander to antiquated patriarchal ideals of feminine beauty; I am doing it because it makes me feel good." What's concerning to us is that, as we age, we are advised in magazines to 'tone it down'; as if we should all go beige and fade into the background as we get older. As if to suggest the fact that we are wearing bright red or pink lipstick is outrageous! But why not go for it anyway, if you so desire and it works for you? Yes, we may need a lip liner to outline our lips more because we have more lines around our lips as we age, but surely that's up to us. We may also need to not wear a powder without a smooth foundation underneath as powder can fall into our lines and this is not the greatest of looks. Or we may need to make our eyebrows thinner than when we were younger to make our eyes look wider. Makeup as we age has to change, but it does not have to turn us into vanilla cake!

So can we still wear false eyelashes for example? We think yes, of course, why not? There are better and better ones on the market now that won't fall off in the middle of a conversation (which once happened to a teenage Livvy, to her total horror as it rested upon the shoulder of her new boyfriend); or you can have them individually put on; or you can dye your own eyelashes so you don't have to wear mascara – there are so many choices, it's very liberating. Which makes Chrissie very happy because, as a teenager she would never, EVER leave the house without her false eyelashes on and now is extremely excited to try all the new types on offer, although not all at once, hopefully!

What about you... are you interested, do you want to experiment? It could be fun. Worst case scenario, it could make you laugh out loud! We wonder why we are sometimes made to feel that it's not appropriate to wear make-up once we are a certain age. Why should that be the case? Instead of harboring the idea that make-up is only for the young, perhaps it is for all of us to help each other be the best and most beautiful we can be and to help us 'put our best face forward' for ourselves and for our own personal confidence levels. And if make-up makes us women look more desirable... this is also the point, is it not? Make-up is not a miracle; it can only boost what is there already. It will not make you look younger but it can certainly improve your image and make you feel that bit more confident and ready to face the world.

Over the years every time we were preparing to go on air just before the radio show, Livvy would have to check and re-apply her bright pink lippy that matched her bright pink nails. Why you might ask? Her reply is this: "I talk differently when my lippies on - more pink and lively" and to "sound fantastic, she had to look and feel fantastic". So much for the myth that radio presenters don't need to look good! It is all about having confidence and presenting yourself to the world. Chrissie's dog is so well trained that he gets really excited when she puts her make-up on and does her hair, as he now thinks it's time for a walk! He knows she would not even dream of going to the park without looking glam. For women our hair is also often a part of our make-up, it is the frame to our face and we can use it in a multitude of ways. It can hide foreheads, accentuate cheekbones and draw the eye to wherever you think would best enhance your face and your best features. We can change the colours to highlight our individual skin tone, which often changes as we age and to make the most of our natural eye colour. Now while we are on the subject of hair - why is it that at a certain age the message is that you have to cut your hair short and put it in a bob? Look, we know that some women really suit that look, but as a general fashion message – ABSOLUTELY NO WAY! Have long hair, have cropped hair like Dame Judi Dench, have dyed hair, have streaked hair, have stylised bed hair (Livvy's favourite). Whatever suits you and makes you feel good is the right hair for you. Chrissie's already got quite long hair, but has a real penchant for some hair extensions. We wear make-up for ourselves to feel fab and gorgeous and much like fashion, we can be as understated or overstated as we like with it. It's your face, it's your hair – love it!

Livvy back in the day

Make Up and Image (Enhancing what you already have)

Chrissie back in the day

Have a go at this exercise to help you become more conscious around your make-up routine.

Exercise 10

Before doing your make up to go out, stop and have a think.

What exactly are you trying to achieve?

Do you want to look understated and subtle...? Or "Let's go for it!"

Be aware of how you are putting out an image to the world...

Make-up consciously.

Go to the mirror. Have a good non-judgmental look at your face... appraise it as if it's the first time you've ever seen it.

Carefully apply face cream and foundation; notice the difference it makes to your skin.

Put on the rest of your make-up, your blusher, lipstick, eyeliner – whatever you wear.

As you do all of this be aware that what you are doing is enhancing what you already have. Allow your natural beauty to be enhanced in this way.

See how you feel…

How do you see yourself now?

Are you expressing who you are with your makeup?

Does it enhance and accentuate your beauty, or does it hide it?

Have you decided at some point in your life to stop and not change how you look?

Have you been defined by the media, magazines, friends and family – or are you looking the same as you always have, since you wore make-up or didn't wear make-up?

Play with different looks.

Buy some new makeup if you can afford it or go to a department store and have a free make-over.

Be bold and tell the assistant what you would like.

At the end of the day, it's about you creating the face you wish to show to the world.

You can listen to this exercise on SoundCloud by scanning the QR code

Chapter 11
Partners, Friends and Family (Or the Art of Fighting Back – Softly!)

As human beings we have a strong natural need to connect to others and to develop trust. It is fundamental to our well-being as humans after all we are by our very nature social beings. Therefore, we work really hard to have friends, family and colleagues in our lives. Our relationships make us feel safe, feel good, feel useful, feel wanted, needed and loved. We have a place in the world, something solid, somewhere to call home; people we can lean on and who we also support and care for. It's a powerful basic need that is reflected in the way our brains are wired and our hormones and nervous systems react and respond.

Once we've built our network of relationships and have taken the time and put the work in to build the trust with the people that are important to us plus seen to our other commitments and responsibilities, what is then left inside for ourselves? The answer is quite often not very much. It can be scary because we love or respect our friends, family and work colleagues and we naturally want to do our very best by them; we really want to please them. But you can't please everyone all of the time, as this can come at a cost to our own wellbeing. When this is happening, we can also find that there is an inner part of us that is dying or disappearing. We can feel claustrophobic, worn out and overburdened by our life. The thing is that as human beings, we also have a deep inner need to follow our own truth, to develop our own creativity, our own sense of self-worth, find our own purpose in life and to live our lives to the best of our ability and to its fullest potential.

You could say that we can feel a need to somehow break free, to carve time and space for ourselves to follow our own inner callings, or just to find some peace in the day. But it's a challenge not to get conflicted, as we know we're so fortunate to have our family, friends and our work colleagues. So to us, the art of fighting back softly starts firstly with ourselves and our primitive fear that if we do something different, or displease any of the people in our lives, we will cause irreparable damage to the relationships we've built up, thereby make our own lives less happy and less safe. It is because when we are perceived in a certain way by our friends, partners, husbands, children and even colleagues, for us to want to be different and to change can rock the boat for them too as they may wonder who have we become. Why are we not happy with things the way they are? Who do we think we are?

We women often think about ourselves in a certain way and narrowly define who we are into a particular box. This can mean that we live our lives from a way of being and thinking which can limit our experiences. We can of course re-create aspects of ourselves and choose to re define ourselves in different ways. By doing this you may discover you have passions, interests and talents you may never have known existed. Other people often don't like us to be too different as it rocks their own sense of security and stability and that is not a comfortable feeling so there can be a pull to make us be who we were before and not to embrace the new, multi-faceted sides of ourselves. As author Jessica Minty points out in her book Codependency: "While it is important to love others unselfishly, it is crucial to find a balance. When we compromise our needs and martyr ourselves to the point of depleting ourselves and neglecting our needs, we become out of balance." This is what we are talking about: how do we get that balance worked out between taking care of the people we love and respect and while loving and respecting ourselves at the same time? Well, it's a juggling act and it's also an art – the art of fighting back softly.

We have worked hard a lot in our lives to create our family, friends and colleague networks, so to disappoint them or not to get their respect and approval as we grow and change is a pretty big, scary and difficult thing to do. We must not take this lightly, as it will press all our fear and survival buttons, but hopefully the desire to explore, to grow and to change things that need changing, is stronger than the fear. We like to believe that hopefully, as our loved ones see that we are becoming more fulfilled and therefore happier, that they will fully support us. So that's when you need to get allies - and this book – to be your companion and together we will face the challenge to be your true creative self and to live your life to its full potential. As Dr. Wayne Dyer so beautifully put it, "Don't die with the music still in you. Listen to your intuitive inner voice and find what passion stirs your soul." It is ok to be a parent and still be sexy and fabulous... to be a grandparent and still want and be allowed to achieve great things in the world... to be a friend and now have new and exciting different interests... to be a partner or wife and want to push forward in our lives and discover new creative pursuits... to develop in your career and to aim for more. The pull is always to be bought back to what was familiar, but we have to be brave. We have to be willing to experience a little discomfort so that we can grow as people. It is hard work at times but the rewards are greater and we are all more alive and fulfilled as a result. As the psychiatrist Thomas Szasz remarked, "people often say that this person or that person has not yet found himself. But the self is not something that one finds. It is something that one creates."

We had both really wanted to expand in our broadcasting career and when the opportunity came to interview the politician the Rt. Honorable Ed Miliband, who at the time was the leader of Her Majesty's Opposition, we thought, well why on earth not? We knew we were a light entertainment show, but we wanted to do a more personal take on him and find out more about the man within and behind the politics. We had a pretty free rein over the guests we invited onto our radio show. Chrissie had initially checked with Livvy to see if she wanted to interview Ed Miliband and Livvy, in her usual positive way, had said "yes, let's go for it". At that point, we had no idea about what we would be up against. To cut a long story short, we emailed him at the Houses of Parliament and he agreed straight away to come on the show. When we informed our bosses that he was coming on the show, it caused a big conflict for them, as they had perceived us as a light entertainment women's magazine show, which we were and this was politics. We had to really fight our corner to be allowed to do the interview. As women of a certain age, we knew that there was an imperative for people to know the person behind the political persona and that this is really important information when you are voting. Well, we had to really stand our ground with our bosses to break out of the BBC 'pink and fluffy' box and show that we could do it, so no pressure there then, when it came to do the interview... hah! In the end, they had no choice but to concede that we did a really good job and, in fact, we did the first ever up close and personal interview with Ed Miliband and we were now seen as interviewers who could do a deep and powerful interview.

Livvy & Chrissie and Rt. Hon. Miliband

This story illustrates well how it can be hard work at times to break out of other people's preconceptions of who you are and what they think you can achieve, be it family, friends, colleagues, partners or bosses. In fact, from pushing outside of our comfort zone we earned a lot more respect from some quarters and also grew a tougher skin which is always useful at work. We think we are all entitled to carry on striving to be the most amazing and fulfilled people we can be without being held back by other people's needs to keep us the same and the fear of us changing and growing. This following exercise is designed to help you to identify any areas in your life where you may be being held back.

Exercise 11

Find a time in your day when you have some space to sit and think. Make yourself very comfortable.

Take some slow deep breaths.

Have a think about your life as it is right now...

Think about your family... your parents... husband... partner... children... grandchildren... your friends... colleagues...

Now - take a moment to get a sense of what you feel like as you see the photo album of your life right now...

See if there is any area or relationship where you feel pulled back... hooked in... made smaller... made invisible in your role... or kept in the familiar...

Imagine what you would feel like to be your own size and follow your own personal journey...

Access the feelings of having a life where you were free to follow your dreams...

Now's the time to work on having your own personal dream and still be in your relationships...

What is your dream... where would it take you if you were to follow it?

Let your mind meander...

Allow yourself to feel what it is like to have complete freedom to follow your dreams...

Really get a sense of what it feels like to have that freedom... let it wash over you...

When you are ready, take some deep breaths and open your eyes.

Write down any goals or dreams you have. Look at them every day and imagine yourself achieving them.

Start to take small but definite steps forward into being who you are.

Partners, Friends and Family (Or the Art of Fighting Back – Softly!)

You can listen to this exercise on SoundCloud by scanning the QR code

Chapter 12
You are Knowledgeable

As we live and survive through the passing decades, we do pick up a lot of knowledge and experience along the way, quite often in spite of ourselves. However, admitting that we do know a fair bit about a lot of things takes some confidence - and definitely takes some practice - but we think that as you get older it is time to acknowledge what you do know... because basically if we don't own it now, when will we ever own it? It is not about standing still though, as we need to both acknowledge what we know and also to keep learning as we go. Knowing and acknowledging that you know a lot, is also knowing that there is so much more to learn! It is important to keep doing things that inspire and motivate us and - very importantly - to get out there talking to people of all generations as there is so much more to learn and also so much to pass on to others.

The Dalai Lama has been quoted as saying: "Share your knowledge, it is a way to achieve immortality"; and Margaret Fuller, the groundbreaking American journalist, author and women's rights activist wrote that "If you have knowledge, let others light their candles in it." We know that it can be really hard to acknowledge what we know and to really believe in ourselves, believing that we do know stuff and have wisdom to offer the world can be very daunting. Sometimes it's a lot easier just to stay small and humble! But if you do that, how can you pass on all of the knowledge you have gained? So what is it that stops us from owning our knowledge? Are we afraid of sounding arrogant if we speak out and say what we know? Do we get scared of people's possible reaction and think they might try to put us down in some way? Knowledge isn't just received and it can also be challenged. It's certainly not nice to be knocked down by people who want us to stay small and insignificant; it can make us feel as if we are 'putting our heads above the parapet', which can then feel like we may get 'shot down'. But actually, we need to really fully own our knowledge, because there is always someone out there who could really benefit from it.

It's a good exercise to think about whom in your life wants you to be the size you really are, who isn't threatened by you being as knowledgeable as you really are. These people are your allies. At what age are we going to say: "I know stuff! In fact, I know TONS! It is my truth, it is what I've learnt in my lifetime, in fact it is my legacy and I am damn well going to OWN IT."? To own your knowledge, to come from a place of expertise and confidence, you have to be strong. It is a form of psychological muscle training – and like any muscle training it's all possible, but you do have to practice. We must all begin to use our expertise and not hide it; the future generations will certainly need it. The more we use it, the stronger we become, the more fluent we get and the better we feel about ourselves. One simple and effective way to do this is by sharing our knowledge with others. Remember that not everybody knows what we know!

Ask yourself these following questions: "What is my gift? What are my skills? What are my attributes? What do I know?" Everybody knows something. From identifying a weed from a flower and knowing what soil is needed to grow a certain plant; to knitting a blanket; to baking an amazing cake; to writing a story; to painting a picture; to fixing a car; to putting up a shelf; to helping someone through a difficult time; to rocking a baby; to knowing how to parent; to doing a budget; to talking about politics, computers... the list is endless! We all have something to offer that other people can learn from. At the BBC, we had no budget for assistants, which we wanted and needed as our shows were very fast and very busy, with guests coming in and out all of the time and we needed lots of help to keep things running smoothly, as Livvy was very busy presenting and Chrissie was busy with the desk. The way we got around this was to find and offer local media students the opportunity to come in and work with us on the show; it really worked for them as they leant how a live radio show worked in practice, which is very different from in theory. They were able to watch and learn from everybody involved in the show and for us this was a win-win situation, as we would also get the help we needed, plus it was really great having them there, they were so enthusiastic, fun and talented. We would encourage them to do things such as going out and about doing interviewing and recording pieces for us to use, so that they could get front-line hands-on practice. Of course, they all ended up with great CV's and a foot in the door at the BBC. We always made sure that we introduced them to the right people and most of them have gone on to have careers in media because of this – one is now at BBC Radio Four; another, Anika, has gone back to her native Sweden and is working at the main broadcasting company there.

Talking of Anika, our wonderful Swedish assistant, we've got a great memory of her from when we met and interviewed the legendary Roger McGuinn of The Byrds. She was taking a photo of us all together on the stage at the local theatre where he was playing and she actually moved his hallowed guitar in order to get all of Livvy's leg into a photo! A great photo versus many thousands of pounds worth of guitar? Obviously, the photo won! There was a sharp intake of breath from his entourage as she did it, but she was experienced with guitars and it was safely placed slightly over from where it was, so that Livvy's leg could be seen and we got a great photograph. What a brave woman.

Livvy & Chrissie and Roger McGuinn

Livvy & Chrissie and Roger McGuinn

Another one of our media students, Duncan, actually came on air with us quite a few times, as we had developed a funny skit that made the most of his dour Scottish humour. Our boss just loved it and used him for work on another show! We have found our students everywhere and anywhere, from chatting to waiters and waitresses in cafes and finding out they, or their partners, were actually media students, to people we knew who had children who were studying media at university. There is always someone who needs to know what you know. There's a danger though, that as we get older, that we can stop learning and just stay where we are with what we know and what we did in the past. It's definitely a dance between owning what we already know and finding out and admitting what we need to continue to learn, as in order to keep our minds healthy and alive we need to keep acquiring knowledge - we all have a constant need to develop and grow, to stay engaged and mentally active. Henry Ford once said, "Anyone who stops learning is old, whether at twenty or eighty. Anyone who keeps learning stays young. The greatest thing in life is to keep your mind young." It is without doubt really important and also essential for our wellbeing. A number of studies now show that if we keep our minds active there is significantly less chance of developing dementia as we age. We may not all be able to afford to sign up for courses of course, but we can read, take up a hobby, watch the news, listen to the radio, meet people for coffee and a chat, anything at all to keep us plugged in and switched on! One of the biggest factors that they have found in keeping the brain youthful is socializing. A study conducted by researchers at University College London found that people who socialised more with their friends at the age of 60 were significantly less likely to develop dementia later in life. Just another reason to get out and get involved in the world.

This exercise will help you to discover what you already know, but may not admit to yourself and also what you don't know and wish to explore further.

Exercise 12

Lie down somewhere comfortable.

Take three deep breaths... one in... one out... one in... one out... one in... one out...

Allow yourself to relax deeply...

See yourself in a library... the high walls are stacked with beautiful books on every possible subject... some you know and some you don't know.

See yourself surrounded by the books... smell the books... breathe in the atmosphere of learning and knowledge...

You are Knowledgeable

Allow yourself plenty of time to walk around the library browsing through the books... enjoy their different sizes... covers... lettering... textures...

As you walk round, you are drawn to two books in particular... they seem brighter and shinier than the rest... you want to reach out to them...

Allow yourself to reach out and take them off the shelf, one by one...

Put them gently onto a nearby desk and look at them carefully...

Really notice their titles...

Now when you are ready, take three deep breaths and open your eyes...

Write down the titles of the books...

Why have you been drawn to these two books...

Now use these titles to think if there are any courses, books, trainings or other learning opportunities that you may want to explore...

Make a decision to act on it, either today or tomorrow.

You can listen to this exercise on SoundCloud by scanning the QR code

Chapter 13
Being Grateful

What does 'being grateful' actually mean? It's a phrase that is thrown around so easily and yes, we know it sounds clichéd... so 'New Age'... but happiness really does come from being grateful for what we have got. It keeps our spirit alive and our confidence strong. We all know that this is so easy to say... and we also know that achieving it can be really, really hard on a bad day. We thought that it might help to get back to basics and have a look at what being grateful is and what actually happens to us when we feel gratitude.

Being grateful is an actual emotional response to something that is good, that touches, moves or inspires us and that we feel appreciation for. It has been shown to chemically change our mood and makes us feel better about our life. We even – get this – become happier when we practice being grateful. We know you are saying "Really?" but the proof of this pudding is definitely in the eating. You have to try it to find out. It's a fact. Neuroscience has shown that focusing our attention on the things we are grateful for creates a shift in our brains and we actually begin to stimulate more neurotransmitters - specifically dopamine and serotonin - which promote good feelings of happiness and contentment. Because we then feel good, we are more able to participate in daily activities that nourish us and make us happy, so it's a self-perpetuating cycle. Being grateful happens when we stop and actually just be appreciative and thankful for this very moment... for what we have right now... but rarely do we do this it seems, as often we're so busy seeing what we don't have and thinking about what we want and what is missing in our lives. Madhuleena Roy Chowdhury says that "Gratitude improves interpersonal relationships at home and work (Gordon, 2012). The connection between gratitude and happiness is multi-dimensional. Expressing gratitude not only to others but also to ourselves, induces positive emotions, primarily happiness. By producing feelings of pleasure and contentment, gratitude impacts on our overall health and well-being as well".

Gratitude is an emotional response that happens in the present moment. Having said that, we can look back and reflect on some of the amazing and lovely things that have happened to us in the past and that we feel very grateful for and by doing so we can bring that feeling back into the present moment to enrich our current lives. When we feel full of gratitude, we become shiny and bright and we want to share it with other people and then they also feel gratitude in that moment - and so the world becomes a better place for us all to be. It's the 'glass half full, glass half empty' syndrome... we can actually choose which version we want to have in our lives.

As Joni Mitchell famously sang: "Don't it always seem to go that you don't know what you've got till it's gone…" So appreciation of what we have now is absolutely imperative. And not being too entitled helps, something a lot of us unknowingly suffer from. Chrissie once had a shower in the flat where she was living that she constantly complained about because, as far as she was concerned, it was "pathetic", "useless" and "not up to the job". It wasn't until she went to a hot, humid country and had to spend ten extremely sweaty and sticky days without any shower or bath, that she appreciated how very lucky she was to come home to a working shower and have fresh, clean running water. That first shower on coming home was the best one of her life and she has never complained about it again. So, we need to really get in the habit of practicing gratitude, because then, like all habits, it becomes a natural part of our daily routine, bringing with it all the benefits that appreciation has been proven to bring, such as increased well-being, better health and happier stronger relationships. Chowdhury also says that "simple practices like maintaining a gratitude journal, complementing the self, or sending small tokens and thank you notes can make us feel a lot better and enhance our mood immediately. Couple studies have also indicated that partners who expressed their thankfulness to each other often, could sustain their relationships with mutual trust, loyalty and had long-lasting happy relationships".

The good news is that when we feel grateful, it is like putting money in the bank and saving it – our bank balance is building and we also get added interest. The same facts can apply to practicing gratitude; the more we are grateful for, the more we put into our 'inner pot' and the more it builds up. In short – gratitude makes gratitude and gratitude makes us happy – what's not to like? But hang on, we hear you say! That's all very well and good when things are going well... but how can we be grateful when things aren't so easy? When our life seems to be one great big fat cosmic joke? Sometimes it is in the letting go of things that we can appreciate what we have in our lives right now. It is really hard to feel gratitude when you are missing what once was. The loss of things and people that are familiar interrupts us and can stop our gratitude. Livvy had a big, beautiful, round oak table that she adored and had enjoyed many a meal on; but when she moved it just didn't fit into her new house. She decided to buy a smaller table, which she didn't really like and she moaned a lot about, mainly because it wasn't her big beautiful table. She freely admits that she had no gratitude that she could afford to buy another table, whatever the size, and no gratitude that she could eat and sit at this new table, or that it fitted her new home and actually looked great. She was just missing her old table that she had loved so much. Then, a few months after she moved in, as we both sat together at this very table writing this book, she suddenly said: "Do you know what? I really like this table! I'm going to let go of my old one, because new stories are being built on this table now and for that I am really grateful." We both then felt really grateful that we could be there together, sitting round her new kitchen table on comfy chairs, stringing words together and drinking cups of tea.

It is most often the simple things that we can take for granted and forget to appreciate in our lives. Hard though it might sometimes seem, if we don't feel we have anything to appreciate or feel grateful for anymore, we need to go right back to the basics and to appreciate the really, really simple things in life. Poet and civil rights activist Maya Angelou suggests this for starters: "this is a wonderful day. I've never seen this one before." And the Buddha is attributed as saying "Let us rise up and be thankful, for if we didn't learn a lot today, at least we learned a little and if we didn't learn a little, at least we didn't get sick and if we got sick, at least we didn't die; so, let us all be thankful." Global peace ambassador and author Prem Rawat says: "And all you have to do is then remember that which is important, that which will produce gratitude—not confusion and anger and fear and doubt—but gratitude, because a heart filled with gratitude will dance."

In our lives we can be grateful if we have running water... a toothbrush... a chair to sit on... shoes to wear... something to eat... a breath in and out... the list is endless. Without gratitude we forget how lucky we are for the simple things in life.

Remembering those things... living abundantly... is awareness that our life is so really rich in so many simple and wonderful ways. This in turn enables us to have compassion for those whose lives are not so rich in that moment - and perhaps inspire us to do something to help cheer them up, like make a phone call... drop by... say hello... make a donation. One of the most inspirational - and hilarious - interviews we ever did was with Sharon, the mother of a teenage boy called Adam, who had learning difficulties and autism. Adam had recently won a swimming medal in the Special Olympics and they had both come into the studio and he spoke on air. It was such a joy to see her immense pride in her son. She was so supportive of him, so full of love and gratitude for him and so happy that he was able to compete in the Special Olympics and to speak on the radio, that it was a totally humbling experience. When she described to us her excitement when he won his race – she said she "thought that her boobs were going to hit her in the eye" as she was jumping up and down so much – we knew exactly what she meant, both as mothers and as women with large boobs!

And here's the thing: when she came back home after the Special Olympics and found that no swimming club would take her son... what did she do? Being the woman that she is, she started her own swimming club, that's what she did, so that her son and other children like him could experience the thrill of competitive sport. Glass half empty or glass half full? She made her choice and her glass was flowing over!

Livvy with Jason Gardener MBE at the Special Olympics, Bath

Here's a simple but powerful way to make gratitude become a daily habit for you.

Exercise 13

It takes 30 to 60 days to implement a new habit.

To learn to be grateful is a commitment to repetition - you need to do it every day.

We suggest you take 10 minutes every day for 30 days - 5 minutes in the morning and 5 minutes in the evening - to write down five things that you are grateful for.

They do not have to be big things – small, simple things are fine like... I'm grateful for running water... I'm grateful for my toothbrush... I'm grateful that I have a brain that can be negative... I am grateful the sun is shining...

Find your own ones that work for you.

Repeat them to yourself throughout the day.

Do this for the full 30 days.

Once the habit is formed, you will want to do it naturally.

Continue the exercise after the 30 days for as long as you like!

We recommend this one as a lifelong practice.

You can listen to this exercise on SoundCloud by scanning the QR code

Chapter 14
Age and Wisdom

We do get wiser as we get older, in spite of ourselves, by the experiences we have had; each experience is a teaching and we can certainly grow much wiser from them. We human beings are exceptional – we know so much. Through all of these decades, from being a helpless baby, we have learned to walk, to talk and to feed ourselves; from a young age we've learnt about relationships, which we are constantly refining and trying to understand; we have learned to read and to write; we have learned lots of different subjects; we have put so many things into practice in the world, from our home life to our working life. We have definitely become wiser.

Wikipedia describes wisdom as the ability to think and act using knowledge, experience, understanding, common sense and insight. Albert Einstein once said: "Wisdom is not a product of schooling but of the lifelong attempt to acquire it." In one sense we are like the Oak tree growing and growing and becoming bigger, stronger and taller; spreading our branches far and wide and growing acorns that drop on the earth – our wisdom is the acorn that becomes another tree with even more acorns. And so our wisdom goes on and on forever. Wisdom is knowing you have survived and lived until now – through all the heartache, the laughter, the pain, the joy, the anger, the passion, the loneliness, the creativity, the numbness, the life-force... and here we are, still standing.

So the time has come to face our lives squarely in the face and say: "Ok, what's the lesson now? When I look back through my lifetime, would I do anything differently? People of a certain age often say: "I am this way!" We say: "You WERE that way... habits can be changed." Another way of looking at it, is that real wisdom is the ability to choose to do something differently. We now have more hindsight, with the years behind us, and so we can see more clearly our past behaviours which may give us the ability to make the choice to behave differently now and into the future than we did in the past. The positive use of hindsight is a very powerful tool... not to be used as a stick to beat yourself up with, but as an opportunity to look and consider whether you could have done something differently. Maturing allows us to critique ourselves without being overtly and harmfully critical. Or as Oprah Winfrey says: "Turn your wounds into wisdom."

Wisdom is learning from your life experiences; we think that a great anecdote for this can be seen in the classic film, Groundhog Day, starring Bill Murray as the cynical weatherman Phil Connors, who for unknown reasons, is forced to live the same day over and over again until he finally gains some humility, appreciation and wisdom. Not to mention falling in love with the gorgeous Rita, played by Andie MacDowell. One very memorable scene from this film that repeats many times is where he walks down the road in a hurry and he steps off the pavement into a deep water-filled hole. He does this over and over again each day, until finally one day he remembers and steps over it! Eureka! That is wisdom. He has at last learned from his – cold, wet and unpleasant - experiences and gained the insight that he needed to step over the hole. Wouldn't it be great if we could learn wisdom without making lots of mistakes first though? Oh well, dream on! Isn't it the so-called mistakes that show us another, better way to be in the world? Who said life isn't a learning experience? Every day there is a new opportunity for us all to develop and to grow.

Talking of wisdom, we once had the privilege of interviewing the renowned peace builder Dr Scilla Elworthy, who has been nominated three times for the Nobel Peace Prize. Scilla was an adviser, along with Nelson Mandela, in setting up The Elders, an influential group of people who work behind the scenes using their accumulated wisdom to end conflict in troubled areas around the world. We can't mention all her achievements, as there are just so many of them, apart from saying they are still coming! But one interesting thing is that she actually began her peace career at the age of 13 when, after watching a news item on TV, she packed her bags ready to go off to the warzone she had seen on the news to see if she could be of some help. Luckily her mum stopped her then, but she hasn't stopped ever since. Now in her seventies, she says that she "couldn't imagine retiring…. it's completely out of the question!" and that her respite is "growing vegetables and flowers, especially roses. It's like nourishment straight from the earth." Memorably, Livvy asked her how people could decide who or what they should give their time and support to when there is so much going on in the world that is crying out for help and she replied: "Go with whatever breaks your heart." That is a wise woman. She also advised meditation as a way to gain inner strength and clarity. We can all gain wisdom and when we do so, we can then decide how to use it to make a difference to our own or to other people's lives.

Dr Scilla Elworthy and the late Archbishop Desmond Tutu

Here's an exercise to help you decide where you could perhaps benefit from doing something differently in your own life.

Exercise 14

It is now time to take a good look at all the different aspects of your life!

Go somewhere peaceful.

Take some space to really think about your life.

Make sure there are no demands on you at this time... look on it as a kind of me-time.

See if there are any areas where you have consistently repeated certain behaviours or habits that may not be serving you in your life right now.

Is it at work...?

Is it with family...?

Is it in relationships...?

Is it around money...?

Is it around your health...?

If you notice any area or areas where you feel that change is needed, now is the time to think how you might achieve that change.

This is not a moment to feel bad, or to beat yourself up, or to have regrets.

This is a moment - using your very own hard-gained wisdom – to decide that you can change, and now may choose to change, how you are in your life now.

Be kind to yourself, change can take time.

We are right behind you.

You can do it.

You can listen to this exercise on SoundCloud by scanning the QR code

Chapter 15
Surviving Loss (And Moving on Gracefully)

In the school of life, we have to learn to survive and to endure loss. Loss is a fact of life for all of us at some point; and of course, as you get older it's pretty certain that you are going to have experienced loss in some way. Surviving loss is one of the hardest things we have to do as human beings, but surviving it does create emotional muscle – we get stronger and more focused about how we wish to live our lives. Clarissa Pinkola Estés, the author of the famous book 'Women Who Run With The Wolves', wisely wrote: "the best land to plant and grow something new again is rock bottom. In that sense, hitting rock bottom, although extremely painful, is also the ground to sow new life on." Loss can come in many forms - through death, divorce or estrangement; the loss of our dreams; the loss of a cherished pet. It can be a loss of trust through betrayal or some other infidelity. It can be a financial loss, the loss of a home, or of a career. It could be a loss of health. So many things come and go in our lives over the years and, unfortunately, if we allow ourselves to love them then we are going to mourn the loss of them. It is what makes us human after all.

The first few lines from the famous passage on love from The Prophet by Kahil Gibran reads: "When love beckons to you, follow him, though his ways are hard and steep. And when his wings enfold you yield to him, though the sword hidden among his pinions may wound you. And when he speaks to you believe in him, though his voice may shatter your dreams as the north wind lays waste the garden." It sounds pretty awful actually – why should we even bother? Why should we not live our lives like islands, not really connecting with anybody or truly loving anything? It would be far less painful that way! Well, that is definitely an option and many people do, or at least try to. But eventually even the toughest nut will usually crack because let's face it, we're just not made that way. We almost can't help ourselves. We humans love to love. We love to connect and share our lives with others. Our whole society revolves around it really, the music, the stories, the films, the marriages, the messages of togetherness. We have always looked to each other for love and comfort, not to mention having children and a family. Our abundant care and concern are not just limited to people – we love things, we love our pets, our abilities, our freedoms. It's what makes the world go around after all! And yes, all of that is really great until loss happens. Then it's definitely not so great; in fact it is totally devastating. It's unbearable. You then wish you'd either become - or stayed - an island. If in the midst of grief anyone dares say to you: "Oh well, better to have loved and lost than never to have loved at all", you want to hit them over the head with something very very hard. Or at least say or think: "Oh really, is it? You try it then and see how you like it", even though Tennyson's optimism with that phrase does give us hope that it is better to have loved than not at all; what we find is it's all about the timing of when it is said. It's what many people think or say when a marriage or partnership breaks up and you are left wondering how you are going to survive it and rebuild your life; when your whole world has been tipped upside down and your dreams are all smashed to pieces. When you're left thinking: "I didn't expect this... this wasn't where I was meant to be now... I thought we were in this for the long haul." Well, certainly our useful motto - to remember every day - is that the best revenge is to have a happy life. But we know it is tough, very tough and so tough it often feels like we can't survive it at all. Happiness seems like a distant dream, a feeling never to be felt again. But with all that said, we can get through it, we can survive it. That's the first thing to know. We do have that capability as humans to survive loss. If you are in the midst of loss right now it might not feel like you will ever get through it at all, that you can ever be happy again and find some peace of mind, let alone joy. But you will.

Vicki Harrison described grief as, "like the ocean; it comes on waves ebbing and flowing. Sometimes the water is calm and sometimes it is overwhelming. All we can do is learn to swim." This is also a time to re-evaluate your life and decide what is important to you. Livvy had four losses one after another, over a period of three years. What has come out of it for her is a desire to live her life to the full... to be happy and to walk away from things that do not fill her with joy. This is the message that she lives by now. For her loss reminded her that she had a life to live well and she damned well is going to live it! As the author J. K. Rowling has said, "rock bottom became the foundation on which I rebuilt my life."

A recent book by the Anthropologist Long Litt Woon, called "The Way through the Woods - on Mushrooms and Mourning", charts how her search for new meaning in life after the death of her husband led her to undertake the study of mushrooms and how foraging in the woods led her not only to peace and happiness but to a new career, new friends and a whole new beginning. Nature is a great healer, as is that highly underrated word: FUN. It seems such a small word both in size and in meaning and feels almost too trivial to mention but actually we humans need to have fun and play, as much as we need bigger, more highfalutin-sounding words with bigger meanings, such as purpose and fulfilment. It's a well-known fact that high stress levels can negatively influence our hormones and neurotransmitters (especially cortisol and noradrenalin) and also affects our endocrine system, metabolic and immune functions; all of which have a negative effect on our mood. One way to naturally balance our hormones is to engage in a pleasurable physical activity. In other words, to have some fun! So take a few minutes and have a think about what fun looks like to you. There are so many ways to have fun, to bring some enjoyment back into your life. Make it the priority that it is. From being in nature, to swimming, to joining a social or sports club, or a walking group, find something that you find fun and really enjoy and get moving. Get those hormones back into balance. Eat well and sleep well. It doesn't have to cost a lot to eat healthily. Make wholesome food from scratch, even if it's just for you now. Look after yourself. Bake yourself a cake, or paint your living room, or raid the local charity shop for a new look, because your creativity is another really, really important element to bring back into your life – or to find for the first time if it wasn't in your life before now. Again, creativity can come in many different forms and it's no coincidence that some people take up writing, gardening, art or some other form of creativity to help them through their loss and help them to move on. It's almost as if fun and creativity can, temporarily at first but more and more and for longer and longer periods of time as you do it more often, lift you out of your grief or loneliness into another state where you don't feel it - or at least you're feeling something else as well, something warm and alive. And in that state, you may even smile or laugh again, or even feel happy again for a while. In time this new happy state will grow and grow the more you have fun and use your creative side, until you can begin to see that there is life and possibly even happiness after loss, after all.

We once spent a day at a local hospice for a radio piece we were making on death and loss and it was such a truly moving experience. It wasn't at all a dreary, sad place, although of course sad things happen there, it was a lively, happy place with all sorts of fun things going on. There were hair salons and art rooms and beautiful gardens and so much love and care and – despite the nature of the place – a lot of happiness and laughter were present. All the nurses listened to our radio show as it made them laugh out loud. Happiness and hospices go together! Johnny Flanagan, who works there and was showing us around (and who knows EVERYONE and seems to be in charge of EVERYTHING, although we think it's actually mainly the PR and fund-raising, which is of course really important, as everything that happens in the hospice depends upon it), is a hilarious, upbeat, larger than life character who clearly loves his job and being with everyone and it is totally infectious. We had a real laugh there – unexpectedly – and also heard some really moving and life-affirming stories. We went back there again with the legendary saxophonist Pee Wee Ellis, who played to the patients and the staff. They really loved it and so did we. So there is laughter through the tears and hope through the despair and we can survive loss and come through it wiser and with a deeper, more profound understanding of life and a greater empathy and compassion for others going through it as well. We can then use this greater understanding from what we have experienced to help others in their time of need, which in turn also gives us something back – a sense of purpose and worth. Johnny Flanagan did exactly this. He told us he took this highly prestigious job at the hospice after the loss of his sister. He is a ray of delightful sunshine to the point where we all three decided that, when the time comes, we'll go together because we will laugh our way out. So there are gifts to be found in loss as well, hidden maybe, almost invisible in fact, but they are definitely there, just waiting to be discovered.

Livvy & Chrissie and Johnny Flanagan of St Peters Hospice

Livvy & Chrissie and Pee Wee Ellis at St Peters Hospice

Exercise 15

Choose a safe space… light a candle… close your eyes…

Breathe deeply in and out three or four times…

Now is the time to make these statements to yourself:

"It's time to come back to me... myself... this is my own journey".

"We come into this world alone and we leave it alone... what is my life about?"

"What is my own journey...?"

"Where do I want to go...?"

"What do I want to see...?"

"What do I want to experience...?"

"What do I want to do in this life...?"

Breathe in and out several times

Now open your eyes

If there are any answers to your questions, write them down

There may not be the first few times, but in time there will be.

You can listen to this exercise on SoundCloud by scanning the QR code

Chapter 16
Sensuality (Flirting with Life)

Cats demonstrate sensuality so easily in every move they make... they stretch, they move with grace and with power. We know that it can be easy to get less sensual as you get older, so... enter Catwoman of a certain age! The trouble is that sensuality is very associated with sexuality and of course that's a no-no for us women of a certain age, we're supposedly not meant to feel sensual or sexy, or be sensual and sexy, or even think sensuality or sexuality in any way! Sensuality is also historically considered to be a bit, or even quite a lot, on the 'self-gratifying' or 'self-indulgent' side and something to definitely grow out of or to hide. Really? Also, sensuality (and flirting, which we'll come to in a bit) have both been co-opted and defined in a male orientated, patriarchal way, often through religions, as being sinful, immodest and definitely not something that any woman should be, do or experience. But our sensuality as women is imperative to connect with a time when we can experience our life force surging through us, firing up our hormones, enlivening and stimulating us. It helps keep us young, vibrant, creative, amused, entertained, lusty and passionate for life and we need it even more as time passes. To define the difference between sexuality and sensuality we need to consider what sensuality actually is? Sensuality is described in the dictionary as the condition of being 'fulfilling to the senses'. Smelling, tasting, seeing, hearing, touching and feeling are the ways in which we use our senses. But what does this really mean in practice?

Well, as we're sure you know when we feel sensual, we get a warm, happy, glowing feeling, we feel good in our skin and we love things that feel good ON our skin. It makes us purr like pussycats, all on our own. Livvy loves getting into bed with clean white sheets. That does it for her every time. Lots of things can make us feel sensual if we allow it - when we're having a lovely bath with gorgeous aromatic oils, or a relaxing massage for example, or having our feet licked by the dog, or our toes swished in the sand on the beach as the tide comes in, or our hair gently brushed by someone else (this is one of Chrissie's favourites). You can get all poetic about sensuality, like C Joybell C:

"The fragrance of white tea is the feeling of existing in the mists that float over waters; the scent of peony is the scent of the absence of negativity: a lack of confusion, doubt and darkness; to smell a rose is to teach your soul to skip; a nut and a wood together is a walk over fallen Autumn leaves; the touch of jasmine is a night's dream under the nomad's moon."

Each of our senses can be aroused, not just touch - we can find things visibly sensual, such as great art or beautiful scenery and audibly sensual, such as wonderful music. Gorgeous smells can get us going, as in the poem above. It's a sense of feeling alive, sultry maybe and definitely sometimes pretty damn sexy as well. You feel stimulated, tingly, aroused and open to connection and hey - if there's someone you fancy having sex with then, great – but that's definitely not a requirement.

This brings us on to something which is very connected to this experience and is just as misinterpreted and misunderstood – flirting. Flirting is also associated with sex; basically, it is generally considered that if you flirt with someone it is as if it's a prelude to having a sexual relationship with them. Well, we think it's time to reclaim it and define it differently, in a woman-friendly way, as well and so we say: "is it flirting…or is it being friendly? Is it wanting to have sex with someone… or is it wanting to connect with someone and share a moment with them, feel an exchange of energy, or laughter, or love and be nothing whatsoever to do with having sex with them? Is it, in fact, a kind of flirting with life?" Flirting with life… we like that, it sounds wonderful. But what does it actually mean? Well, it is a fact that, as human beings we have a need to connect, to share our time in this life with others, to communicate and to be noticed. Loneliness comes from that connection not happening and it is proven to be potentially fatal. Bottom line is that we need other people. So when you are friendly to people and having fun, communicative and compassionate; fully giving them your attention for a moment or a few moments, this generates a sort of electricity that passes between you, as you experience an emotional and energetic link - and that is flirting as we see it.

We think you can flirt with anyone and everyone; the cashier in the supermarket, the man walking his dog, the people in the restaurant, children, older people, younger people, men and women. Not just your partner (or potential partner anyway!). Flirting can happen anywhere. To us, it's just about being an alive human being who cares for and is interested in other human beings. They feel it and get something from it and so do you. It's a win-win for all. It is also about loving life; about feeling the life force flow though you and knowing you are a free spirit, a 'wild woman' who 'dances with wolves'. Well, not literally of course, but you get the drift – let go for a bit, come alive and enjoy a bit of sensuality, a bit of flirting. Hone your skills, try it out. We bet you're a lot funnier and entertaining than you ever realised. And remember - it doesn't mean anything more than you are a fabulous, fun and friendly person with a great view on life, unless you want it to, of course.

The problem is that there is so much ageism around flirting per se. You are allowed to do it when you are younger but not allowed to do it when you're older, so it is said. So, at what age should you stop?

You know what we're going to say, don't you? NEVER, of course. Talking of which, we had an outrageous flirt with the Stranglers bass player and spokesman JJ Burnell once, when we interviewed him over the phone. It started off hilariously when Chrissie, channeling her inner Barbara Windsor in full-on 'Carry On' mode, informed him she was just 'tweaking some knobs' to get the sound right, to which he obviously made an equally rude double entendre and it all went downhill (or uphill, depending on your viewpoint!) from there; in the interview when Livvy asked him about his martial arts training, he invited her to "come and feel his abs anytime". We all cracked up laughing and obviously she accepted his offer! Who wouldn't, he's still gorgeous after all? Unfortunately, on the one day he was able to come into the studio, we couldn't make it but hey ho, in our dreams eh? We told our editors some of the conversation and they definitely weren't impressed; in fact, they looked fairly horrified and gave us a "that certainly wasn't very BBC, was it" look. But the thing is that not only was it great fun - something important to have at work always - but it actually made the interview much better as well, as he also talked emotionally about being in France during a terrorist attack and how it had affected him; we think that because we had bonded with him over a bit (well a lot) of flirty banter he was able to then open up to us a bit more. It certainly livened up our day anyway and hopefully his too– always good to feel you've still 'got it' at least. It's no coincidence his parents are French either, as the French are definitely the experts at flirting.

Look, we're definitely not saying that flirting is all about double entendres or sexual innuendo, or indeed anything sexy at all of course – although it can be - but more so it's about just having a bit of fun with someone, male or female, old or young, whatever it is fun looks like to you. Having a laugh and showing a genuine interest in someone can be enlivening and invigorating, not to mention entertaining and we all need a bit of that. Giving someone your full attention and interest and really listening to what they have to say, can be received as like you are having a sensual bath together. It's a kind of sharing of your inner light, your energy. A celebration of sensuality… flirting… passion… life… joy. It's what keeps us going… it keeps us alive. And if we've lost it, for whatever reason, then we need to find it again. It's our line to life… our lifeline if you like… and we need to hang on to it. Sensuality… flirting… being outrageous… they are all part of being a woman of a certain age and living life to its fullest potential, as far as we are concerned!

Livvy & Chrissie – flirting with life!

Here's an exercise to help you get in touch with your sensual and flirty self.

Exercise 16

Take half an hour out for yourself, in a quiet and private space. Put on your most comfortable and sensuous clothing… find textures that are lovely to the touch.

Sensuality (Flirting with Life)

Find a beautiful rug, duvet and velvet pillows... whatever makes you feel like saying "Mmmmmmm".

Light two candles and have a lovely scent in the air, flowers or perfume.... whatever makes you go "Mmmmmmm" and feel lovely.

Close your eyes and allow yourself to breathe deeply into your chest...

Allow the breath to deepen into your tummy... feel the rise and fall of your breath... in and out...

Become aware of your skin and the shape that you are... now draw an imaginary line around your whole body, so that you know where you begin and end...

As you breathe in and out, notice a golden flame inside of your tummy and your womb...

As you continue to breathe in and out, notice that the flame increases till eventually it has become a warm sun...

Allow the golden glow from the sun to encompass your whole body...

Now let your body move, stretch, wriggle... like a cat!

Feel the texture of the rug and enjoy the sensuous pleasure that it gives you...

When you are ready, take a few deep breaths... and open up your eyes.

Take the warm glowing feeling with you out into your world.

Be alive!

You can listen to this exercise on SoundCloud by scanning the QR code

Chapter 17
Sex it up (Reclaiming your Sexuality)

There is a myth that women of a certain age are not into sex and are glad it is all over... well, we beg to differ! We are railing against stereotypes all of the time and let's face it, whether you are into sex or not, who wants to be placed into that kind of a box... who wants to be told that? Isn't it about time we connected with our own sexuality and decided what we think for ourselves - not what we are told we should feel about being sexual women? There are so many negative messages out there, as if it's not okay for women to be sexual and it's only men who have the privilege. Well, we definitely think there is room for both of us. We also think the conditioning gets even stronger as we women get older. As you know, we're not interested in being put on the scrapheap, so we think that it's time to reclaim that which may have got musty and cobwebby and stuffed in the attic by society. It's definitely time to get the polish out and give our sexuality a good old shine.

Okay, so when was the last time you felt that 'Zing'... that 'Yes!'... that 'Buzz'... that 'Phwooar'... as you moved around in your day? That's what we're talking about. Owning your sexual energy doesn't mean you have to have sex... it is an amazing energy and it is up to you what you will do with it. It is a very natural and creative life force. Why do you think athletes and sports people are told not to have sex before a race or performance? It's because it is the transformation of their sexual energy into something else - like winning that race - that can energise their performance and give them that edge. Basically, we are all alchemists. Having said that, it brings to our minds the time we were doing the Sport Relief video and we had to go to RAF Brize Norton to learn how to do a parachute jump. Ooooh... very sexy, you might say. Ooooh... men in uniform, you might say. Well, yes and no – yes to them, but no to us. So, imagine... there we were, women of a certain age, great hair and great lippy, looking good in our civilian clothes. But then... horror! We were put in camouflage-covered overalls – slightly baggy, saggy and tied round the waist. Really not a good look! Now Chrissie at 5ft 8inches tall ended up looking not too bad. Livvy at 5ft 4inches tall, Mrs Fashionista herself, ended up looking like a sack of potatoes with huge overalls on and an overly large helmet squashing her fab hair. Not a sexy look, one could say! So there we are, the scene is set and we have never been anywhere with so many gorgeous fit men in white vests and combat trousers, with big, sexy arm muscles, in all of our lives. Helping us to fall... and catching us ("swoons"); and then hanging us from parachute harnesses, where we looked the most unattractive, we have ever looked. Really! This is a time when you want to look fabulous, don't you? Oh well, it was all for a good cause! How do you cope with all that sexual energy racing around your body? Well, we used it to conquer our terror and jump 125ft. And not only that we are now officially allowed to parachute jump from a plane! Hopefully with one or two of those guys helping us along the way!

If we go back in time, women were either the 'Madonna' or the 'Loose Woman' – two labels that have put us in a very difficult position. Men are just sexual or not sexual. So, being women of a certain age, we need to have a middle ground. This doesn't mean you can't cook the dinner, or be a grandparent or a parent, or soothe the burning brow of your ailing partner, but maybe you can then, in the next while, be having a hot time in the bedroom, should you so desire. It's all about connecting with what you want. Can we not have it all? It's time to bridge this gap between one extreme of women viewed as having no sexuality and the other extreme of women viewed as being only sexual and nothing else. So how do you do that, you may ask? Women are not supposed to be sexual, or orgasmic. Victorian women were frequently diagnosed with a condition called 'hysteria' – now considered to often have been sexual frustration. They were treated by doctors with pelvic massage or even clockwork vibrators! The 1950s were a time of very rigid rules around female sexuality. There were 'good' girls, who were marriage material and 'bad' girls, who were definitely not.

We of course have had the whole era of the sixties since then, when it was considered that women should be open to free love. But then again, some were and some weren't - and also some felt they had to take part, even if they didn't really want to. So again another label was placed on us women, that if you weren't into free love, you weren't cool! Then the 1970s was full of women owning their sexuality for themselves, but sometimes, it was done in a way that, while it worked for some women, for others it was just way too extreme. It seemed that this was a time where owning your sexuality meant giving up on the lippy and having your nails and hair done and not shaving anywhere! It sounds great for some women, but maybe not for everyone. So, women of a certain age, isn't it the time to find out what YOU want and how YOU want it, without fear of your own inner judgments kicking off. We say inner judgments, because ultimately, that is what is going to stop you from being as free as you could be around your sexuality; all those myths, stories and beliefs you may have picked up along the way, about how - and how not - you should behave and you should feel.

One of the judgments that seems to be out there is that beautiful women do not have a brain – for example, it transpired that Marilyn Monroe, who was renowned as a beautiful and sexual actress, was also an extremely intelligent woman. Another beautiful Hollywood actress, Hedy Lamarr, was a mathematically-minded inventor. So when we had the opportunity to interview the Chippendales, the famous American male strip troupe, we thought we would turn this notion on its head. So off we went to the theatre to catch the Chippendales before they performed that night. The queue outside was full of women of all ages - lots of hen parties and lots of excitement! We were invited to interview the guys in their dressing rooms, as they prepared for their evening show. Well, there they are, standing there with their extremely well-defined muscles, as they oiled their amazing torsos prior to the show. You can tell these men take bodybuilding and working out to another level! Not quite our cup of tea, but hey, we're here for the interview and while Chrissie holds the mike up close and personal, Livvy asks, in true BBC style: "do you think that women want you only for your body and not your mind and how is that for you?" It was met – unsurprisingly - with no response!

Another time that springs to mind when a response was NOT forthcoming, was the time when, after playing Marvin Gaye's Sexual Healing track, Livvy unexpectedly asked Chrissie – live on air: "Do you do sexual healing, Chrissie?" A horrified silence ensued... followed by a "Well, errr, I might..." from Chrissie. This was followed by lots of hysterical laughter and frantic keeping it together when the next track came on (now you know a bit about what goes on behind the scenes... and the effort taken to pull yourself together when you're back live on the air!). As the author of the book Sex after Sixty,

Marie de Hennezel, says: "As they get older, some people decide to give up on sex altogether. That is their right of course and if it is a mutual decision, then it isn't a problem at all. I believe there is no age limit to love, sex and desire, even if we often hide it after a certain age. It is like a secret that we don't want to reveal, but that plays a key role in the physical and psychological health of older people. We should talk about it more!"

And so, if you need it, here's another good reason to have a healthy sex life – according to research sex does all of the following: reduces blood pressure; lowers stress levels; boosts immunity; helps your mood, relationship and mental well-being; improves sleep; reduces anxiety and – the biggest perk of all as far as we're concerned – it helps you to look younger, because of all the hormones! We say bring it on! And remember... you can use your sexual energy any way you want... to be creative... artistic... competitive... or just to feel really alive – at any age!

Sex it up (Reclaiming your Sexuality)

Livvy & Chrissie at RAF Brize Norton

The Chippendales

Here is an exercise to find out what is in the way of you becoming more sexual.

Exercise 17

Think about the messages that you have been told as a sexual woman.

Write down ten beliefs you have about being a sexual woman.

Think about where you have heard these messages from...

Was it:

Society...?

Your family...?

Your relationship...?

Your schooling...?

Your work...?

TV...?

Magazines...?

Write down where these beliefs have come from.

Now... think about how you wish to change the messages.

Are you going to follow these beliefs... or are you going to make your own decisions about your own sexuality?

Write down what you decide and commit today to moving forward with these decisions.

This is YOUR sexuality and YOU make the decisions!

You can listen to this exercise on SoundCloud by scanning the QR code

Chapter 18
Asking for what you Want (Even though you may not always get it)

If you don't ask, you don't get – that's always been our motto and it still is. Asking doesn't always mean you're going to get it, but don't let that stop you asking for what you want– it certainly has never stopped us! So, to hopefully inspire you to ask for what you want and not be daunted by a mere "no" or two, or even ten, here's some of our more spectacular "coups", as we liked to call them, plus a couple of examples of our general chutzpah and punching above our weight-ness. Remember – if we can do it, you can do it!

Bryan Ferry

We once interviewed Bryan in his very swanky hotel room before a gig. He had a dose of man-flu so Livvy, who suddenly turned into nurse of the year, suggested the best herbal teas for it. He told us he had garlic and manuka honey on him anyway, so he was definitely on the road to curing himself. We then started the interview. We had planned prior to the interview to ask him if we could be the women on the cover of his new album. Why, you might ask? Why not, we say. The interview then starts and it is always stressful to find the right moment to ask something outrageous. So… the moment finally comes and Livvy starts by saying: "So Bryan, you've had a lot of gorgeous women on the cover of your albums... Jerry Hall... Lucy Helmore ... Playboy girls... what about me and Chrissie for your next album cover?" There was a pause... a silence. We interviewers have learnt over the years to just keep breathing and wait at moments like this. Bryan at last responds: "Great - two for the price of one!" Well, that's a bit cheapskate if you ask us... and we're still waiting for the call for the photo shoot!

Livvy & Chrissie with Bryan Ferry

Asking for what you Want (Even though you may not always get it)

Rt Hon. Ed Miliband MP

Amongst a lot of flurry, we had a very prestigious interview booked with Ed Miliband MP, who was then the leader of the opposition. We always worked really hard in advance while preparing for an interview, wanting to get the right questions and not being standard fare, finding something interesting and unusual if we could, that hadn't been heard before. So, in normal 'us' style, we had a cunning plan to ask him a cheeky question. The interview was going really well and then came the moment for Livvy to ask the said question: "So, Ed, it's been said that you would like to see more women on banknotes. You mentioned Emily Pankhurst and some other women of great stature. Well... what about Chrissie and I?" He laughed out loud and said, "Yes, you're, definitely candidates!" He then said that he'd "have a word with the Governor of the Bank of England" and that "we were on the shortlist". We're still waiting.

Sir Nick Clegg

Nick Clegg MP was Deputy Prime Minister when we interviewed him. Now, Nick is a very English gentleman who doesn't give much away, so researching him (with the invaluable help and knowledge of seasoned BBC journalist Kate Adie), we were able to come up with a good set of questions for the interview, plus an outrageous request. We knew he had played drums in his younger years, so to talk about this in an up-close-and-personal interview was very appropriate.

Livvy: "So, Nick, you used to play drums in a band, didn't you?"

Nick: "Yes, I did. How did you know that?"

Livvy: "Well, we did our research prior to meeting you and we wondered when you leave politics, if you would like to join a band with us? You can play drums and we can swan around in the background."

Nick: "Great! We can call it Nick and the Swans... a plan has been hatched".

Even though he's left politics, we're still waiting for the call.

Livvy and Sir Nick Clegg

UB40

We were interviewing UB40 and there is much fun and banter and of course the topic of the song 'Red Red Wine' came up during the interview, as it's one of their most famous hits.

All was proceeding swimmingly well, until the moment we ask:

"So... could we audition right now live on air to be your backing singers on 'Red Red Wine' for when you perform it later tonight?"

They hesitated then said: "Sure!"

We catch our breath and then we sing the chorus of "Red Red Wine" in a live on-air audition. Not too bad, we thought.

There is a long silence from the group.

Then they said: "Absolutely no way."

"So that's a NO then," we say.

Michael Eavis CBE, originator of Glastonbury Festival and Miles Leonard, Chairman of Parlaphone and Warmer Bros Records UK

A PR company invited us to a garden party / fete in Somerset to interview, independently, Michael

Eavis and Miles Leonard. It was an outside job really – there was noise, loud music, children laughing and shouting... general mayhem! Where on earth were we going to be able to get a quiet place to do the interviews? The PR woman was running around like a headless chicken and we were running out of time as we needed to go off to another place. So, in true Livvy and Chrissie style, as we are chatting to Miles, we say "Look, we need to get this interview done... somehow!" Now this is a man who is responsible for the fame of Coldplay, Kylie Minogue and others... and we were running out of time.

Chrissie, the techno whiz that she is, says that a nearby hedge will be perfect as it will muffle the noise. All three of us then dive right into the center of this huge hedge, fighting our way through the branches and leaves! Thankfully, Miles was a great sport and we got a great interview with him... plus lots of foliage in our hair.

Now, we could not ask Michael Eavis, who is in his 80s, to go into a hedge with us for an interview. Luckily, the PR woman ran back just then and says "I've found a bedroom in the guesthouse for you to interview Michael."

"Great!" we say. We walk into this tiny room with an enormous double bed in it, which we are now lolling on, as there are not any chairs. Michael is bought in for the interview and he stops... looks at

Asking for what you Want (Even though you may not always get it)

us... looks at the bed... looks at us... and gingerly sits on the end of the bed.

By the end of the interview we are all relaxed and chatting, but the whole day goes down as some of the strangest places to interview someone.

So, it was two Yesses!

We got the interviews - and with a decent sound quality.

Livvy & Chrissie with Michael Eavis and Miles Leonard

Jingles

We very cheekily asked and got, lots of very famous people to do jingles for the show for us. We got great jingles from JJ Burnell of the Stranglers, boyband JLS, reggae band UB40, soul singer Smokey Robinson, singer Bryan Ferry, actor Anthony Head, Mark Millar (from DIYSOS), Roger McGuinn (of the legendary band The Byrds), John Craven (Countryfile), Carol Cleveland (of Monty Python fame) and singer Elaine Paige, to name a few.

Well, get us - radio presenters with big stars doing jingles for us!

After all, if you don't ask, you don't get.

Exercise 18

Your mission, should you choose to accept it, is to ask for something you want – however big or small it may be, however outrageous.

You may get it – but then again you may not.

At least you would have tried. And you may get something else even better.

And remember - if we can do it, so can you.

Good luck!

Chapter 19

Shock, horror, it's not only going on in media!

We often talk about our own experiences in the media world because that is where we come from and we believe that changing the way that women of a certain age are represented in the media will really and truly impact all women across the board. However, this phenomenon certainly isn't limited to the media world and so we have asked other women to share their stories with us, so that we can see what life is like for women of a certain age in all walks of life.

Here are a few stories that we collected:

Keeping on learning - Pamela

As a very successful and creative business woman, who had a thriving business that didn't need too much attention from her anymore, four years ago Pamela decided to go back into academia in her sixties. As she says: "I decided that I had reached a stage in my life where I wanted to spend my time on deep work and thinking. I decided to do a Masters at University as I already had a Science degree. I chose to do Philosophy and soon discovered that it was a very male dominated department. As all of the other students and most of the lecturers were much younger than me and as an older woman, I felt like the ultimate minority group! As I progressed, I decided that the life of the mind was where I wanted to be working at this time of my life and I had a desire to really explore some issues in a solid scientific and critical thinking way so I decided to apply to go on and do a PhD. This was when one particular lecturer said to me: Why would you want to do that; you've already had your career?" "This really blew me away - it was like a slam down. What it felt like was that this is not a career that I can take on at this age. How could I possibly have time in my life now to develop a new career?"

"I think when we're younger there are all sorts of beliefs of how we will be at a certain age and stage in our lives... and it's only when we get to this age that we truly realise that the glass ceiling is partly within us... from the beliefs and expectations that we held in the past and our own lack of confidence and so when you come up against someone else's limited beliefs about you, it's like there are now two of you in the room limiting you." Pamela completed her Masters last year and has put in her PhD application. She has also just done a film making course so she can make a film on her research!

Risking giving women a voice - Deborah

Psychologist Deborah worked for a large international organisation based in Geneva for a long time mentoring and coaching the female staff. Just before she left, she was asked why she thought the female staff were not going for the higher positions within the organisation. Deborah says: "I thought it was probably something about the culture, but I agreed to ask the women why they felt they couldn't progress... how they felt about the culture in the organisation... what was holding them back... lots of general questions like that." She talked one-to-one to a cross section of the women there and the feedback was that "the culture was like an 'old boys club'... even after they left. They came back and kept things as they were and the women felt very angry about this but did not feel they could do anything about it." The men who were around in this organisation were in their 50s, 60s and 70s or older and there were no women working there over 55. This was because "it was an organisation that men felt incredibly comfortable in and it was hard for women to get in on the conversations. The men would go off and have the conversations and the women couldn't find them or join in and so they didn't have access to the information they needed." Well, Deborah of course wanted to feed this back to the managers but was blocked by the male Head of HR who refused to believe what she had found, as it wasn't his experience of the organisation. However, Deborah went ahead with a high-level meeting and presented her findings somewhat anxiously as he still challenged her and tried to publicly humiliate her and discredit her findings. Then something happened; the women who had been previously too intimidated to speak up came to her defense: "What was great then was that the women who had been interviewed actually stood up and started to say that they had been interviewed by me and that I was sharing their experience... and that it was true for them... and those women had some credibility in the organisation and so he had to back down".

"I think that being a woman of a certain age gave me the confidence to do this... because I thought in one way, I had nothing to lose... I'm going to share this truth. If they don't like it... if they stop employing me, it's not the end of the world, it's not going to define me and I will at least have the sense that I spoke something that had great importance for the women in this organisation. "It felt really important to say it. And so, I did."

Going for a new life - Janet

Janet was a full-time wife and mother for most of her life and after her marriage broke down leaving her as a single woman of a certain age, she has been left pondering what that meant for her. One thing she struggles with, she says, is "knowing what my status in the world is. If you're married, however it might be, that is your status... and as I'm past child-bearing age, how do I fit in the whole dating, mating game now?" Janet said she finds being single in her sixties is hard as there is "no-one to watch your back... and no-one to eat with". She also thinks that "the loss of the hopes and dreams I had for this time of my life... such as being with my husband and enjoying the grandchildren together", now leave her having to rebuild a new life for herself, one she never thought she would have to do. She also feels that, that as a single woman of a certain age, she has to "defend her corner more against all the narratives about her, such as what she should be doing, what she should be feeling and how she should be living her life".

She also thinks that her friends want to fix her up with a partner albeit in a well-meaning way but it's just not what she wants right now. Bravely, she has recently moved across the country to be nearer to her daughters and some good friends and is now living in a small, close-knit town where there are lots of opportunities for getting involved in community life and meeting new people and she really is enjoying the feeling of independence and freedom and of being her own woman... and she doesn't rule out the possibility of another relationship in the future!

The Musicians Story – Lyn

Lyn entered the music profession in a big way in her forties. When her husband's rock band needed a singer she sneaked off, took singing lessons and joined the band! Being in her forties and fronting a heavy rock band, she came up against a lot of interesting attitudes including one man saying "how lovely of you to carry your husband's gear in for him..." and one classic remark: You're not young, you don't have legs up to your armpits... you'd be better off doing something else." As she says: "the men rock and rollers can be enormous and ancient... but women definitely can't!" She thinks that more women artists coming into the industry will help change attitudes although she says she noticed that the older generation of men rock fans "still have a mindset that women should be in the kitchen!" Lyn is still rocking on as a duo with her husband but is looking at forming an all-women rock band and is currently working with a female promoter to put on a music festival for women of a certain age.

Leaving the corporate world to follow her heart - Geraldine

Geraldine, who is now 60 years of age, had spent most of her working life in the centre of the hectic corporate world of banking in central London. She was very good at what she did and earned a substantial income, having worked her way up from the bottom; it had not been easy and inside she yearned for something more meaningful and fulfilling, as she did not feel she got this from her career. At 50 she decided to sell up, leave her job and everything she knew in London and move back to a beautiful quite rural area in Ireland that she had always loved and she would now be near to her sister also. She then decided to retrain as a life coach and has spent the last number of years working with teenagers who are troubled and with adults to help them explore their authentic selves and how they can bring that energy to the world and use their natural gifts and passions to make a living. She also met her husband in her 50s not long after returning to Ireland something she had belived she was too old for and would probably never happen but it just goes to show that there is no such thing as too old. Geraldine said that for her becoming a woman of a certain age in many ways freed her from the stress of expectation she had felt in the corporate world to constantly climb the ladder and succeed. "It was a very male dominated environment" she says "I had to work twice as hard as the men to prove myself despite my results being generally much better than my male peers, and at some point I just stopped caring about the nonsense definition of success and thinking about what success would really look like for me and this had nothing to do with money". Geraldine said, "I encourage all woman of a certain age to get out there if at all possible and start living the life they really want as time won't stop for you, even if it is only small changes that you can make you and your happiness are worth it". Geraldine said she spends a lot of time in nature now and really enjoys gardening and is learning an instrument - something she had always wanted to do. She has even gotten so good she has played in some traditional sessions.

The Camper Van – Liz

Liz had been married at 19 and was 9 months pregnant with her fourth child when, one winter's day, she found herself up a ladder hanging wallpaper while her husband, as usual, was sprawled on the couch. As she did all the hard graft and listened to him snoring she heard the words her father had said to her many years before: "love is blind and that fella wouldn't work if you plugged him into the mains". It had taken her 5 years but she decided that day to throw him out of the house and said, "since she was doing it all on her own anyway it would make very little difference". Liz worked hard for the next 18 years raising her family alone and trained as a primary school teacher. Now 63, with her kids all grown and some with kids of their own, she decided to use her savings and buy herself a fabulous VW camper van to start travelling any chance she can get. She said she especially loves going to music festivals. She has since been around a lot of Europe in her van sometimes alone sometimes with her friends or family but as she says herself, "I was born for the nomadic life and I sure am going to make the most of this chapter of my life". On being a woman of a certain age Liz said, "in ways I feel less invisible now than I ever have. I spent so many years in tracksuits, run ragged raising my wonderful kids, and now I have time to look after me, to make the most of my looks and to dress how I want and have fun. I have just recently met a great man and so far its all going well but with or without him I am going to enjoy life. I even did a basic car maintenance course last year so I could look after and maintain the van myself when I am travelling".

Developing confidence in life - Catherine

I am a 68 year old R.G.N. who has worked in hospitals abroad and in U.K. For me the most important asset that one can have in order to succeed in this life and in old age, is confidence. Having confidence makes one feel strong and able to cope with life's vagaries more easily. I believe this also has a positive flow-on effect on other life enhancers and parts of my life. For example, having the confidence to know what is a proper and healthy diet, staying a healthy weight, taking regular exercise, developing interesting and beneficial hobbies, making enjoyable social interactions and relationships, coping with financial worries, never feeling 'invisible', managing ageing, feeling happy with one's 'looks' and finally, staying positive. Achieving these outcomes in life, for me, came down to three tough life experiences. The first one was as a child in a Roman Catholic Primary School. The second was as a thirteen and fourteen year old teenager being forced to assist in the building of a two-story brick house and the third was as a twenty four year old challenging a Senior Surgical Consultant on the negative effects of him smoking in the staff office. Primary school was, for me, a very anxious and hurtful time. The teachers were cruel and unkind. However, when I left for secondary school I began to question and think more deeply about the awful effects of their teachings. As a mature adult I decided to act and seek satisfaction by writing to the relevant bishop to enquire why the Catholic Church allowed their staff to treat children in such an abhorrent way. The response was an admission of a wrong and an apology, I was happy to reply that that was all I was seeking. Stepping-up and challenging the wrong-doers was a huge flip for my confidence. The second profound experience involved my father. He insisted during the summer school holidays that I assist him, along with my two brothers in building our two story brick house. I was not happy. I wanted to go around town looking for boys to play with. When I matured I enquired of my father as to why he made me do all this building work, blocking, bricking, slating, mixing cement, sawing timber, putting in sewer pipes etc. He replied that I would now be competent enough to build my own house! It is true that as I weaved through life I have been able to tackle most issues of a practical nature on my own. Confidence was building up... The final experience I know gave another boost to my confidence was really quite difficult and unpleasant, but, it had a very successful outcome. To put it briefly, a surgical consultant I was working with in a busy hospital smoked heavily in the staff office. This was detrimental to the health of the staff and any clients that were in the close vicinity. One day I challenged him on this serious issue which resulted in my being called into a meeting (with a witness). I was questioned as to why I thought I had the right to challenge him about his smoking in 'his' office. He was my boss and he had a right to smoke there if he so desired. I swallowed hard and slowly and carefully replied that he was a danger to our health, that it was wrong to smoke in a hospital office and, that he was a poor role model as a medical consultant. The final outcome of this meeting, at a future date, was the consultant admitting I was right and that he could not help himself. He agreed with me that if he continued smoking then his future and demise would be very painful. In conclusion, the secret to survival as I see it comes down to confidence in oneself, the confidence to step back, assess the situation, take your time, know your rights and finally succeed. Once you have these tools in your 'pocket' ageing will be a breeze.

Amba's journey in fashion

Amba is a stunning black woman from Gloucester UK; she has always had an outrageous and colourful fashion sense – from her gold lamé trainers to her leather trousers, sparkly platform shoes, and shortish skirts. Amba's relationship with fashion goes way back. She says: "my mother was a seamstress… and she was always making things for me… and I think it just stemmed from there… and then as I grew up I wanted to make my own sort of fashion, one could say, so I took a Saturday job to fund my fashion addiction. As far as I can remember I've always loved clothes... and colours... experimenting with different ways to wear things."

Livvy asked her what her experience was now she was a woman of a certain age – did she feel like she needed to alter in any way how she presented herself to the world, was it different now?

"Yes, just slightly... a lot of things that were above the knee I've got rid of... my dress length is a bit below the knee now... having said that, not if I'm on holiday.... or it's the summer. Actually, thinking it through, in the winter I wear thick tights with shorter skirts as well... so maybe I do wear shorter skirts still, but with a nod to over the knee sometimes!"

We asked her how she felt people now related to her being fabulous and a woman of a certain age...? "Well, I get a lot of compliments.... People want me to take them shopping. I do feel that I can't wear my outrageous shoes all the time ... I've moved into flatter shoes...partly for my back... but sometimes I just throw caution to the winds and wear what I feel... I notice though that I think more about it now... I used to just wear something without thinking about it... and now I'm thinking 'Shall I...shan't I?' 'Can I... can't I?".

She says: "You hear this voice that says "mutton dressed as lamb...", where does it come from? Somebody will say something to me, like the other day when I had my gold chunky trainers on and my leather trousers and a 25-year-old said to me "Wow, look at you!" and for a second I had to think 'what am I supposed to think… what does she mean by that? Is it because of my age… I'm sixty… that I'm wearing it and looking okay?' She really meant it as a compliment, but for a second I'm thinking - is this okay… should I be wearing this at my age?"

She goes on to say: "I'm no size twelve – I'm a big busted, full-figured woman and this year I've bought some cycling shorts which I wear with a big tee-shirt. And I can wear them with a little short dress if I want to kick my legs in the air!"

Livvy asked her if she thought her Jamaican cultural background meant she could be more her sexy, sassy self, at any size, and Amba agreed: "the men I know don't want bony women – they ain't vegetarians, they like a bit of meat!" We had a good laugh at this!

Amba has had a big life to date, and you would have thought she would have gone into fashion but no, she started out working in admin at a national gas company and progressed to taking projects to the city - always dressed amazingly, of course - and taught young girls how to use computers.

Amba was a mentor at a local school - still looking blingy of course - and received a teaching qualification from the University of Leicester for changing a young teenagers life around by talking to him and helping him believe in himself, something she did naturally as a woman of a certain age. She is still outrageous, and still determined to strut her stuff, now with a huge dose of empathy and life experience. For Amba looking good and doing good is a given - you can still help people and look fabulous. It's her motto!

The Personal Trainer - Lynne

Lynne is a vital, energetic powerhouse of a woman. She has been a personal trainer since her children were at school, as she needed to find a job that fitted around her life. She worked hard and gained her fitness qualifications and now she heads up Yeofit, a gym situated at the beautiful Yeo Valley HQ in the stunning Somerset UK countryside. So women of a certain age can be fitness managers and trainers, and inspire us all!

She is passionate, in an infectious way, to get us moving. We had her in the studio over the years on the radio... if you imagine people being talked through exercises on air - it worked! Obviously, she made us both do it but Chrissie could usually manage to avoid it - typically - as she was doing the desk, but she was always happy to volunteer the assistant we had in her place... really?

Lynne encourages movement as a way to keep fit and strong as you get older. "Just get moving!", she says, and "If the issue's in the tissues, then motion is the lotion" and "rest is rust".

Lynne says she hears people say: "Well I'm sixty now…" and I think: "So what? I've got people coming to my classes who are in their sixties, seventies, eighties, and nineties. I've got a woman who's 78 doing weight training and lifting 20 kilos."

There are plenty of people in their sixties, seventies, and onwards still doing my mainstream classes and definitely keeping up."

So where does this message come from that as we get older we need to get more careful and delicate, and therefore more sedentary, we asked? Lynne says that it's a fact we do lose muscle fibre as we get older but that it is a sedentary lifestyle that does it, not ageing; she says it's our convenient-type lifestyles which make us more unfit by being sedentary - it's now easier to get to the shops, we buy our vegetables rather than physically growing them; we watch TV, we sit on the sofa more, so we now do less exercise, and therefore we're not so strong.

Keeping strong, Lynne says is really important to keep injuries at bay from falls, and also for preventative measures, because your muscles and joints are stronger and more flexible, and your reflexes faster. Also if you do need an op, keeping strong and fit beforehand can really help your recovery.

And to prove it, Lynne herself has undergone surgery four years ago for a back problem she had had since childhood and is now weight training, running, and doing everything she did before. She says that her surgeon was spectacularly pleased with her progress after the operation because she kept strong and fit beforehand, instead of taking it easy as she could have, therefore recovering faster.

She says that weight training and Pilates are best for keeping strong and toned and help combat the loss of bone and muscle fibre, but she also says that any progression is good if you're sedentary, so going from sitting to standing and then from standing to walking, running, to exercise classes - anything is good as long as it's in the right direction! Then we can progress to weight training which is brilliant for all the joints and muscles and can help keep at bay osteoporosis. Of course, you need to work with an expert like Lynne.

Lynne says that it's not dangerous to do exercise but that so many people believe that it is and are scared of it; she is incredibly reassuring and knowledgeable.

She says: "It's just a good time now, after the Menopause, to get strong, and it can even lengthen your life! It's our insurance policy for later."

Shock, horror, it's not only going on in media!

Exercise 19

'Now it's time to write down YOUR story. Do share it with us at: yourstory@scandalofsexit.co.uk'

"All the chapters in the book lead to this moment, to this time. We need to find the courage, strength and tenacity to live the life we choose. Choose it now"

Love Livvy and Chrissie

Book Club Page

This book is perfect for a book club, as you can share the thoughts and insights that this book has hopefully inspired within you. The exercises are something that you can share as a group. Here are some ideas of topics for you to ponder on if you fancy:

1) What did you like best about the book?

2) What did you like least about the book?

3) What was your initial reaction to the book?

4) What feelings did this book evoke for you??

5) What was your favourite quote or passage?

6) If you had a chance to ask the authors of this book one question, what would it be?

7) How original and unique was the book?

8) What did you already know about this book's subject before you read this book?

9) Did the book change your opinion or perspective about anything? Do you feel differently now than you did before you read it?

You can start your own book club, find an established club near you, or you can find book clubs on-line.

www.ingramcontent.com/pod-product-compliance
Lightning Source LLC
Chambersburg PA
CBHW050020130526
44590CB00042B/1121